THE DIVORCE

Tori Lynn

Copyright © 2013 by Tori Lynn

Printed in the United States of America

ISBN-13: 978-0615961330

ISBN-10: 0615961339

All rights reserved. No part of this book may be reproduced in any form or by any means without prior written consent of the publisher, except in brief quotes used in reviews.

The names and some specific details have been changed to protect the identities of individuals.

Book Design and Production by Contact Lynns Publishing
Front Cover Graphic Designer by Ronny Myles
Editing by Tamara McCullough

Most of the Bible scriptures in this book have been quoted from the New International Version (NIV); these are other versions that were used.

King James Version (KJV)
New Century Version (NCV)
New Living Translation (NLT)
American Standard Version (ASV)

Contact Lynn's Publishing
www.jerrilynnspeaks.com
www.authortorilynn.com
972-850-8858

ACKNOWLEDGMENTS

My Heavenly Father, Who I later realized was there whole time, thank You for turning my mess into a message. Thank you for **shielding me** from death *and* **keeping me** in my right mind. YOU ARE I AM.

To Apostle Robert E. and First Lady Kennetta Lee (my second parents): Apostle, thank you for SHOWING me what **unconditional** love <u>is</u>; and how a dad **should** love and support his daughter. First Lady, you have to share **your husband** with the world and keep him lifted, yet be a First Lady of the church, a wife, and a working mother. Thank you for your strength, courage, empathy, and testimony.

To my daughters paternal grandparents and aunts, thank you for always being there for not only the girls, but for me also. When everything went crazy, your love for the girls remained the same. I love and thank you for everything.

Thank you Rico and Debbie Allen, Tracy Hamilton, Rosolayn Johnson, The Garners, Faleasha Tate, Sister Spence, Sylvia Lucas, Christine Aminisaber, Leah Bryant, Linda Patrino, and Zoya for holding my hand and **demonstrating** a Christian love walk. There were moments that I could not see God, but I felt Him through you.

Grandma Ponds, you ARE LOVE. I have always known that I hold a special place in your heart. I can do no wrong in your eyes. I pray that God give me the wisdom and unconditional love that a parent should have for their child. Dementia has you but, I have your heart. I love you dearly and miss us.

To my mom, Author Jerri Lynn, and my sister, Ronyea Thompson, we have had our trials and tribulations, but in the end, we **ALWAYS** have had each other's back. Mom, thank you for checking in when I checked out. Surviving three BRAIN SURGERIES lets us know God is a Healer and a Restorer. Mom and Sis, I don't know if I have told you this but you two are the most amazing women that I know.

Last but not least, to my brother (son) and my daughters: after all we have gone through, love, laughter, and sacrifice for "mommy" is what has gotten me through these years. You all are my Angels and I, through you, am learning patience and unconditional love.

TABLE OF CONTENTS

Introduction   1

THE BEGINNING

1. The Crush   3
2. The Battle: I Want Sex   12
3. The One Night Stand   15
4. Meet The Parents   24
5. Fired?   18
6. My Dear Mother   19
7. I Didn't Need A Man   21
8. The Relationship   24
9. The Ex   29
10. Before We Wed   32

THE MARRIAGE

11. If It Could Go Wrong, IT DID!   36
12. I Married My Best Friend   44
13. The First Argument   48
14. Power: Given Or Taken   52
15. Fired Or Quit   54
16. The Understanding   56
17. In Front Of Our Children And Friends!   59
18. The Arrest   67
19. No More Excuses   73
20. Anger Against The Wrong Man   75
21. Airing Dirty Laundry   78
22. Fired Again: Pole   82
23. Fired Again: Chicken And Dumplings   85
24. The Thought Was Nice But…   87
25. Our House Guests   90
26. Fired Again: Gas   92
27. Fired + Arrested = Labor   96
28. The Crumble   102
29. Postpartum Depression   106
30. The Families   108
31. But, He Was My Husband!   112
32. Together! Again???   116
33. Unusual Behavior   119
34. The Day Of Mom's Brain Surgery   121
35. The Church   124

TABLE OF CONTENTS

THE SEPARATION

36. Pregnant, Alone, and Heart Broken   127
37. Although It Was A Bad Idea   129
38. The Day of Excitement, Or Disappointment   131
39. John, John, JOHN!   135
40. The DAY ARRIVED   138
41. Delivery and Drama   150
42. Drama Before Discharged   179
43. Mama's Baby, Daddy's Maybe   153
44. The Church: Again   161

THE DIVORCE

45. Filing For Divorce   196
46. Guess Who Came To Court   198
47. Meet Our Daughters   172
48. How DID I Get Here   174
49. Finally, It's Over!   178

Introduction

My mom has been married and divorced three times and bore three children within those marriages; and me, the second to the oldest, she bore in a non-married relationship. She was the head of the household in those relationships and owned the home that she had built, when I was two-years-old, and where we lived for twenty-two years. She owned a successful janitorial business that paid the bills; her established credit bought the cars that she and her last husband drove.

I, myself, now have been married and divorced twice. In my first marriage, my ex-husband and I moved into his parents' home, with them. The six month marriage ended in divorce with no children. In my second marriage, I owned the home that my husband moved into with my brother and me; my successful business and established credit bought the cars that we drove. The marriage of nearly two years ended in divorce with two children.

On our wedding day, before God and man, my husband happily promised to love, honor, cherish and respect me until death do us part. Later in court, before God, he told me,

"Watch your back because I'M GOING TO KILL YOU!"

The Beginning

CHAPTER 1

THE CRUSH

It was a typical warm Sunday in the fall. My mom and I had visited a church we used to be members of before we moved out of the area. We walked through the doors of the sanctuary that was preparing for the second service, and there he was. Standing close to the pulpit talking to another member, was a handsome, six feet two inched football-built, broad-shouldered man wearing a double-breasted, three-piece navy suit, grey shirt, silver cuff links, navy and silver striped tie, and leather navy shoes.

"Mom, look at the usher down front," I said.

"Ooh, Tori, he's cute! Let's get closer," she responded.

Mom and I began to walk down the aisle towards the front of the sanctuary. While looking for a place to sit, I remembered a time when I had heard a CD, from a single's ministry conference, of a famous minister and relationship doctor telling singles that it was okay to show some sign of interest while at church. **SO**, as soon as we were close enough, I walked in front of him, slowed down my steps, and looked straight into his eyes to be sure he understood that, *I am making eye contact for purpose of interest.* POW! Our eyes locked. He stopped talking in what looked like mid-sentence. As time stood still, there was a connection between us; it was as if no one else was in the sanctuary. His eyes followed mine until finally I turned away and continued to find my seat. I didn't see where he sat during church, which was good, so after church, I asked mom if we could hang in the lobby until he finished serving, but he never came out so we left.

I was a successful hairstylist and I rented a suite in a very prominent area. For a month, I asked random people if they knew who this handsome walking doll was. It didn't matter the nationality; I had to find this guy. Chloe, a hairstylist who had a suite down the hall, came to my suite with good news, "My boyfriend use to go to that church and he knows your guy!"

Four months later, now winter, I visited the church again, this time with Chloe, who was excited about her first time visit. On the way there, she had gotten a flat tire and her boyfriend came and changed it. This made us late, but we were blessed because the usher was able to seat us fairly upfront. Maybe thirty minutes later, instead of focusing on the message, my eyes surveyed the usher seats and, BINGO.

"There he is!" I whispered to Chloe.

A few seconds later, Chloe said, "Tori, he knows you're here!"

I asked her how she knew because every time she would nudge me, he had already looked away. She said, "He keeps looking at you."

Then, finally, I caught him. He would look over, then look away, then I would look over, then look away. During this brief game of eye tag, I thought, *Oh my goodness, this guy is gorgeous.* I don't remember how long the spirit of distraction had us, but eventually, I quit playing and tuned into the message.

After the benediction, Chloe insisted that I approach him:

"Tori, go talk to him!" she said.

I replied, "GIRL, NO!"

"This is the new millennium; women are asking men out now," she tried again.

"Not me. I'm old-fashioned." I said.

"C'mon, c'mon, this is the guy you've been talking about!" she insisted.

I finally agreed, but we looked around and he was gone.

We went to the lobby and stalled because I understood that he was serving and had to stay in the sanctuary until it was clear. I killed time by chatting with **every** old member that I knew. Then, finally, he came out. My heart began to flutter with excitement. *This guy is a DOLL!* I thought. Once again we made eye contact. He walked back and forth speaking to **everyone** around me and talking into the mic in his sleeve.

April, a client that I ran into, and I were conversing when I finally looked over at the guy and told Chloe, "He's not approaching so he must be in a relationship."

April asked, "Are you talking about that guy in the navy suit?"

Chloe answered, "YES!"

April looked back at me and said, "Tori... he is beautiful."

The two of them began to convince me, "Tori, he is nervous, he may not know what to say, just wait a few more minutes."

April and I continued conversing when suddenly, Chloe went missing. Fearing the worst, I looked around; yes, Chloe was talking to the guy. My heart fell into my stomach. I got nervous. My breaths were becoming shorter and shorter. I felt as if my underarm pores opened up and began to angrily eat my deodorant. I thought, *what is she saying to him? She is messing the whole pursuit thing up. He is supposed to find me...*

She returns chipper, "Hey, he likes you! He's coming to talk to you!"

Elbowing her in the arm, I said, "GIRL! OH MY, YOU ARE NOT SUPPOSE TO.... Hi!!!"

He was there, standing right in front of me. The girls immediately disappeared.

With an amazing smile and lips that had just been Carmexed, he introduced himself, "Hello, I'm John."

I looked up at him and said, with a cool demeanor but an intense EXCITEMENT buzzing on the inside, "Hi, John, I'm Tori."

I nearly fainted because not only was he stunningly gorgeous, but his eyes were an amazing hazel green.

"So, are you single?" he asked.

"Yes, you?" I asked.

"Yes. You are very beautiful and single? What's wrong with you, are you crazy?" he asked.

Shocked, I responded, "Well, you're handsome and single, are **you** crazy?"

He responded, "I don't know. Would you like to find out?"

"Yes!" I answered almost interrupting him.

He asked for my number and I gave him my business card. He told me he would call me later that evening.

Having only been in the car for maybe five minutes, my phone began to vibrate. I looked down to find a number I did not recognize.

"Hello?" I answered. It was HIM!

"Hello, Tori, this is John." I knew it was him for he had me at "Hello" inside the sanctuary.

Ecstatic, I took the phone away from my face and looked at Chloe while pointing to the phone with my mouth screaming but no words coming out, "IT'S HIM, IT'S HIM!" Chloe snickered as I returned calmly, "Hi John."

That conversation was the best forty-five minute ride home. Chloe was on her cell phone telling her boyfriend the great news of my meeting John, while I was on my cell talking to John.

At one point, during her conversation, she was no longer excited. She became silent, seemingly listening intently to what her boyfriend was saying on the other end. Then she said, "Yeah, I will talk to her but not right now."

"The One"

My conversation with John started around 12:00 that afternoon and ended around 8:00 the next morning. He was encouraging, a sweetheart, and FUNNY. John was a security officer at a library, volunteered as usher in the church, was the father of a two-year-old daughter. But, he lived at home with his mom.

His reason, "I moved back to help my mom take care of my grandma."

That could've made sense until I asked, "Is she sick?"

He answered, "Oh, no, she died two years ago."

My thought was, *TWO YEARS AGO? Did I miss something?* (Red flag)

That afternoon, he called and we met at a Mexican restaurant for lunch. We had a great time laughing and talking. Towards the end, I told him I had just bought a house and was having problems putting up the wood blinds. He offered to help and followed me home. On my way home, I called my mom, who lived in Plano, TX, less than ten minutes away, to tell her that I was having the guy, that I have been having a crush on, over to put up the blinds. John had put the blinds up but not without breaking the edge of my desk from standing on it. It was cool; at least no one was able to look inside the house while walking their dogs.

Later, we sat on my couch in my den and talked for **hours** on into the night. No television, just us talking. The more we talked, the more I realized that he was not "The One." He began to talk about situations that happened between his mom and her ex-husband and his dad and stepmom. As he talked about it I started thinking, *in his mom's divorces, she didn't protect him and his siblings eyes and ears. They witnessed and experienced too much. On one hand, I understood that she was a hard working mother, but at the same time, she should've protected her children.* He became **very** emotional at that moment. (Another Red flag) Usually when I see a man cry, it breaks my heart and I feel for him; I want to console him, or do whatever it takes to make him feel better, but this time was different. He was **so** emotional. I couldn't help but wonder if he was serious or wanted panties; but the more he talked and cried, it was obvious that he didn't feel protected by his dad or his mom in both marriages. Maybe he was just upset with his mother for the decision that she made to leave his dad after her infidelity, or the choices she made in the marriage to her second husband which also ended in a divorce. However, **both** the divorces had taken a great toll on him emotionally, and now in his 30s, he was emotionally **stuck**.

I had seen that type before. I knew him all too well because of my little sister's dad, my mom's second husband, Willie. Willie would get very emotional and would cry loudly, hit the wall, or walk fast through the house huffing, puffing, and yelling. He was always attached to some type of drama or created drama. Everything was dramatic.

John was nice. He was a gentleman who was FUNNY, caring, and admired me for having custody and caring for my paternal brother, Cameron. I had a bachelor's degree, I was a successful hairstylist, I drove a black Land Rover, and I owned one home in Frisco, TX, and one in Arlington, TX. But, after conversing with John, I realized he just wasn't for me -- he wasn't "**The One.**"

CHAPTER 2

The Battle: I WANT SEX

He carries me into the room. Immediately, I throw him against the door which he just locked, ripping the buttons off his shirt. As we turn and I began to walk him backwards, I unbutton his pants. Then, it's a dream or a fantasy. I had quite often fantasized about my wedding night. Well, I couldn't care less about another wedding, so I fantasized about the honeymoon. Moreover, ending these droughts by Legal Sex, Consummation, Conjugal Cohabitation, Due Benevolence (1 Cor 7:2-5), God's Wedding Gift (1 Cor 6:15-20), "MINISTRY," and best of all, God calls it, "GOOD!" The two spirits and bodies become one (Mark 10:8). Where two or more gather in agreement, He's in the midst (Matt 18:20). He is so serious about the marital sex that He tells us that our bodies are not our own and do not withhold due benevolence. Hmmm, well, hey, I'll be happy to do my part! When I get to heaven, making love to my husband will be the one thing that I won't have to answer for. But right now, I'm single and I'm a believer. I should not be having sexual thoughts because eventually, as Proverbs 23:7 say, as a man thinketh so is he; where the mind goes, the man will follow. I think I have gone past my thoughts. I want Sex. If a man lusts in his heart, he commits that sin (Matt 5:28). At the same time, I know how God feels about fornication and tells us to flee (1 Cor 6:18). I'm not one that can "do it," and then ask for forgiveness just because I know that God is a forgiving God. He says in John 14:15, "If you love Me, you will obey My commands," so I knew that I needed to marry or stop fornicating (1 Corinthian 7:9). So I thought to myself, *I know I will remarry eventually, but when will that be?*

I was molested at three-years-old I don't know if that fact is the reason I had become addicted to sex or because I come from a line of nymphos. While feeding my spirit daily by reading the Word of God, I amassed the strength to stay celibate for years at a time, as long as I stay focused on my walk with Him. I have to avoid temptation by all means. I absolutely cannot even talk about sex since these desires give birth to sinful actions. And when sin is allowed to grow, it gives birth to death (James 1:15). I don't even date. No need in opening that can of worms because it's too hard to go back and close that lid. The pattern is I finally start dating a guy, then nine months to a year later, there goes my mind, then my body. So with my best interests in mind, I try not to date unless I know where this man is going. Hopefully we don't taint the union, or shall I say, "Open the present before Christmas." Proverbs 4:23 warns us to, "Guard your heart, for it determines the course of your life."

I was in an intense BATTLE in my mind: *I want SEX, but I'm a Christian turning into a freak. How do I lift my hands in church and lift my legs at night? God says in John 14:15, "If you love me you will OBEY my commands." Maybe I should get married so that I won't burn with lust. But he's not "The One." Well, if I get married, at least God won't be mad at me anymore.*

CHAPTER 3

The One Night Stand

Since I had just gotten out of a relationship with a guy twenty years my senior where we didn't have sex the first ten months of our on-again, off-again four year relationship, it was only logical to think, *well, since God has been mad at me anyway, I may as well go ahead and do it again.* Although I knew John was not "The One," I decided that I was going to have sex with him, then wish him well.

So while he was still emotional, I was in a head spin, *Is this guy serious or is he doing this because he wants to take my panties home? I'm going to "do it" to him either way, but he's going to have to pull himself together.*

As he continued sitting with his head down, I was getting frustrated thinking, *OH C'MON, YOU'RE TURNING ME OFF JOHN! YOU'RE KILLING THE SWITCH!!! How did we arrive at this dreadful subject of divorce in the first place, and how the heck do we get off???*

After he stopped crying and pulled himself together, he kept his head down and said, "I'm sorry."

I told him, "Yeah, dude, for the future, on the first date, you can't be acting like a… you know!"

We laughed which was good because I didn't want him to leave while he was so emotional and get into a car accident or something. *Plus*, that guilty conscious was on reserve for the sin of sex.

Finally, I guess the therapy session was over and he said, "Well, I'm going to get out of here; it's late."

The ongoing battle in my mind: *Number one, I've only known this man ONE day. Number two, what if he is a believer and has a strong walk with the Lord? He's going to think that I'm an assignment from Satan. If he rejects me and leave, then I will know that he is serious about his God; therefore, he will be serious about his wife. I am totally aware that I am spiritually weak in my walk right now…*

We were standing in the entry of my front door. He leaned over to hug me with those big, strong arms; I was wrapped up in his chest. I didn't let go nor did I want to. It felt so good just being curled up in there and listening to his heartbeat. That long hug turned into kissing; the kissing turned into walking backwards into my dark living room (wow, almost like my fantasy). He braced my back as we fell to the floor. After that, well, you already know the rest. I laid there thinking, *sex him then wish him well-- mission accomplished!* But wait, the sex was unprotected, "John, DID YOU JUST CUM IN ME???"

The Morning After

My mom called and asked how the date went with the guy from the church. I told her that he was a great guy but I didn't think he was "The One." She asked why. I explained how he had not accomplished anything, he had not completed anything, and he didn't have anything. She told me that with God all things are possible, that God can change anyone's situation in a blink of an eye.

The next day, we met up at a place for planned parenting for the Morning After/Plan B pill. Yes, it was pretty embarrassing for me to be a grown woman so careless that I thought about pregnancy prevention **afterwards**. I didn't have to worry about this problem in the previous relationship with the older gentleman. He had a vasectomy because he didn't want more children, which is the reason we broke up. Not only that, but how smart was I to have unprotected sex with a man that I'd only known for twenty-four hours? Was it the fact that if we had stopped to put on protection, that would've given one or both of us time to think and realize that what we were about to do was wrong? The fact I was giving myself permission to sin?

After John paid for that $50 pill, we left. I saw a Chinese restaurant a few doors down and invited him to have lunch with me, my treat. We had a great time. Talking, laughing and joking. We had a blast. That day forward we were inseparable.

CHAPTER 4

Meet The Parents

His mom

On our third evening of hanging out, I came to pick him up from his (his mom's) house for an event going on that side of town. While waiting, his mother came from the back room and introduced herself. She was very warm, friendly and nice. She turned the channel and found an old movie. I sat down and said, "Wow, this is an oldie but goodie." John popped popcorn and we stayed and watched the movie with his mom.

Not long after that day, she began to sit with me at church. After church, she invited me over for breakfast, lunch and dinner. As I mentioned before, we were together every day, either at my house or theirs.

Because John and I spent so much time together for nearly a month now, I finally invited him to come and meet my mom. But on that particular day, she was very sick from a stomach virus, so I told him that we'd have to postpone until another day. He offered to come and help me with her, but I knew she'd die before she'd allow it. I took care of mom the entire day until the illness was too much to handle and I was forced to call 911 where she had to stay in ER overnight for dehydration.

The very next day, I woke up nauseous. My stomach was turning, sounding like a backed up toilet. I had caught the virus.

John called and I told him that I had the stomach bug. He responded, "I'M ON MY WAY!"

I begged him not to come because I had diarrhea and vomiting. I surely did not want him to see me in that condition, especially after having only known him for such a short amount of time. He came over and helped me with everything. I have to admit, he took great care of me. John made sure I ate chicken noodle soup and crackers. He took the vomit trash out and gave me Gatorade. At one point I was in such agony because my body started aching, he ran downstairs and got me salt water to drink. He massaged the Charlie horse out of my leg, rubbed my back, and placed a cold towel on my head and neck. He didn't care about getting sick; he just rested on the loveseat quietly. He stayed with me the entire day and evening until I fell asleep.

My Mom

A few days later, that day arrived. My mom did the mommy thing, asking one million questions at about fifty miles per hour. After the interview, I knew my mom thought the way I thought the first day I met him, *He is not "The one."*

The next morning, I went by mom's house. As soon as she opened the door she began, "Wow, Tori, he is just one big teddy bear. His plans are so way out and confusing. I mean he is just a teddy bear and that's **all**!"

I asked, "Mom, weren't you the one that said that with GOD all things are possible and GOD can change anyone or anyone's situation in a blink of an eye."

Shaking her head, she answered in confusion, "Tori, he's way off. His plans, has he thought anything through thoroughly? I just don't know about him. He is just a big teddy bear and that's all!"

CHAPTER 5

FIRED?

On Valentine's Day, John surprised me at my job with a dozen roses and a beautiful card thanking me for being in his life. When I got off, I surprised him at his job with a teddy bear holding a rose and candy. I knew he had no money so I invited him over where I cooked dinner and rented a movie. It was an absolutely fantastic evening.

A few days later, I asked John what was his schedule for the week. He replied, "I don't think I work there anymore."

My thoughts were, *how in the world do you not know if you are employed or not? Do you clock in or out anywhere? Are you on a schedule? Is there a pay check or stub with your name on it? I mean what in the world?*

Obviously, he had been fired, but I admired his hustle. He began doing little side jobs here and there. I suggested that he to go into business for himself.

CHAPTER 6

My DEAR MOTHER

At this point, John and I were together every single day. Once I finished working, he was headed my way or I was headed his way. One of those days that John was at my house, my mom and sister came to visit.

My mom asked John, "John, tell Shon your plans for opening your own business."

I saw a dark cloud hover the earth. I couldn't believe she asked him that knowing that plan was off. I had not told him about the conversation my mom and I had the week prior, so he had no idea that she was disturbed by him and his business plan. Sure enough, he repeated that same plan to my sister. When John finished, Shon sat there with a blank stare. Mom began to laugh. My sister asked John his business plan again but reworded her question hoping to get a better answer. However, it was the exact same answer from start to finish. This time mom laughed uncontrollably. Now, John was aware that he was the joke. A man who stands six feet two inches sat there as if he were three-years-old. I can still see the look on his face from the embarrassment of being laughed at.

I thanked my mom and sister for the visit and walked them out of the door; mom walked out with tears in her eyes from laughter. I walked back into the den to find John still sitting on the couch. He just sat there. I was sorry for how they had been treating him and for what had just happened, but I didn't say anything. What could I say? He didn't say anything either. I gave him a minute.

While I prepared our meal, I tried to figure it out, *how do I handle this?* **She's my mother.**

My mom is a businesswoman. She is an author, she's owned janitorial businesses and she's cared for over fifty foster children in her home. My mom is amazing and unbelievably smart. She quit school in the seventh grade yet raised three college graduates. Growing up, we always had money, a nice house and nice cars. We, including the foster kids, never missed a beat. Plus, my grandmother, aunts and a few cousins have their own businesses; so we are pretty much aware about what goes into planning, strategizing, expected outcome, cost and so forth. So, when John told my mom his plan, it was obvious he had neither been coached nor had spoken to a business professional about his plan.

The next morning, I went to my mom's house for breakfast and I asked, "Mom, why did you ask those questions in front of Shon? You knew that plan was crazy before you asked him to repeat it and I haven't gone over the plan with him yet."

She retorted, "What does he be thinking? I mean seriously, does he think before he speak? Aren't you embarrassed when you two are out in public and he starts talking? Tori, I know you two have been spending a lot of time together and it seems that you two are very serious, but if you marry him, everyone is going to look at **you** differently."

CHAPTER 7

I Didn't <u>Need</u> A Man

John and I were lying on the couch together one evening watching television. The movie was going, but I had so much on my mind that I could not get into it. I was a bit sad about all the drama I was having with my mom. John had never said anything against her, although I'm sure there were times he wanted to.

Suddenly John grabbed the remote and turned the television off. I looked at him and asked, "Why did you turn the TV off?"

He answered, "You want to tell me what's wrong?"

I looked away shaking my head.

He said, "I'm not going anywhere. I'm not going anywhere. We're in this together." He grabbed my hand and turned my face towards his and asked, "Do you hear me? I'm not going anywhere."

"I don't know when this is going to end, this nightmare," I stated, "You can be with anyone and any family that will be there for you, to support you and not tear you down for being with their daughter. You don't have a chance with me and I love you enough to let you go."

He sat up while looking down. I continued, "You don't deserve this. We come from two different worlds and to my mom, you will never be good enough."

We both sat in silence for what seemed like forever.

John looked at me and said, "Well, I love you, I want to be with you. Besides my daughter, you are the best thing that's ever happened to me. You love me, you believe in me. You love your brother. You are such a strong, smart and successful woman. I don't have anything, but I may die trying to give you the world because that's what you've given me. I don't want to be without you, so you are just going to have to get rid of me because I'm not going anywhere. We'll be just like Bonnie and Clyde."

I looked at him and said, "I love you, too. You make me forget about everything that's wrong and that I can do no wrong. I need that; I need you."

John seemed stunned. He was completely silent. He dropped his head and took three deep breaths.

I asked, "What's going on?"

John responded, "I have never had anyone to tell me that they need me."

I smiled. We both laid back on the couch and I turned the television back on.

He grabbed the remote turning the TV back off and asked, "Will you marry me?"

"Turn the TV back on and quit being emotional," I answered.

"Well, I was kind of serious," he uttered under his breath.

He wrapped his arm around my waist and I placed my arm on his as we held hands. We finished the movie and he left.

A few days later, Saturday, we took Cameron to Oklahoma City, OK to visit the maternal side of his family. While there, we visited The Deliverance Church, my God-father's church. He gave an amazing sermon and ended it with, "If you got in your car and stopped at the light but someone ran that light and killed you, where would you wake up, Heaven or Hell? Do you know?"

Cameron went up and gave his life to Christ. I was all crying and snotty. I could not have been happier knowing that everything I had gone through for and with him that would be the pivotal moment made it ALL worth it.

Apostle called John up and looked into his eyes and began to prophesy to him. He called me up to stand next to John and told us both, "This is going to happen. You two **will** get married."

By that time, I was overwhelmed and I heard nothing else. John just hugged and held me. Then, I felt another set of arms and hands. Both John and I turned and it was Cameron with this HUGE grin. The three of us stood there hugging with joy.

John and I made it back to Frisco and sat in our favorite spot on the sofa. One of our favorite television shows was on. About one minute into watching it, John turned the television off and got down on one knee and grabbed my hand, "Tori, I can't take it anymore, will you marry me?"

He didn't have an engagement ring, so I said, "Cut the TV back on and cut out all that playing!"

"Not joking," he said, "please."

I answered, "Yes."

CHAPTER 8

The RELATIONSHIP:
Blossom AND Wither

My relationship with John continued to blossom as my relationship with my mom withered.

John treated me as if I were the best thing that had ever happened to him. He trusted my suggestions and encouragements for starting his own business and it seemed as if his day would get brighter, just because I was in it. He **loved** to make me laugh, a simple smile just wouldn't do. When you saw one, you'd see the other; we were inseparable. He had my back and I had his. He loved Cameron and Cameron was crazy about him. He had to introduce me to everyone in his world. He was proud of me. I was accepted and loved **unconditionally**.

My mom, on the other hand, reminded me EVERY DAY, "You are making a mistake; you are changing. Your mentality is different, you are beginning to talk different. He has nothing and you are going to lose everything you've worked for. God is not responsible for anything that he did not put together, God is not going to bless you two."

She told me everything wrong with me and my relationship with John. When she saw that our relationship was getting stronger, she doubled the attacks on him. When that didn't work, she moved to his mother.

THE DIVORCE

mom, Mom, MOM!!!

One day mom came by the salon while Brenda, John's mom, was there shampooing my clients' hair. Mom and Brenda began to talk and something went wrong. I know mom asked Brenda about John and his work history because by this time, John was unemployed -- again. Brenda began to talk about her son, who she obviously loved with all her heart. It was all positive as a mother's love would be for her "Mama's Boy." Obviously, the apple didn't fall far from the tree because some of her reasons for why he was having a hard time staying employed was unreasonable even to me. But of course, I was NOT about to entertain my mom with it.

Finally, mom went in for the kill after Brenda, who **was aware** that my mom and I were having problems in our relationship, began to say things like, "Well, I try to support my children. If there's something that they want to do, even if I don't agree with it, I just let them do it and I will just be there for them. If there was a pothole at the end of the street, I wouldn't warn them; I would just let them fall in it. I don't try to interfere with my children's lives."

OH NOOO! I once again saw the dark cloud hover the earth.

My mom quipped, "Are you advising me? Are you seriously trying to tell me how to raise my children? I have three college graduates and one in high school who is in the gifted and talented program. My oldest is a Major in the Army. Tori, as you see, is a very successful homeowner and business owner. And my other daughter just graduated from college with Honors and in the top 10%! And you're trying to tell me how to raise children?"

Brenda sat there in shock with her mouth open.

Mom continued, "That's what I thought, so please, PLEASE don't attempt to tell me how to parent because obviously you've done something wrong with all of your children, especially with John, who won't keep a job!"

Oh, my God, I could not believe it. Brenda had nothing to say. She stood up, hugged me and left. Shortly after, my mom, totally undaunted, left also. I had no words. I cleaned my suite and left.

Once I had gotten to my car, I sat there for about five minutes imagining how Ms. Brenda was feeling. I was torn wondering, *why is my mom doing this? It's okay to do that to me but not others.*

On my way to John's house, I called and briefly told him what had just happened.

The attacks were so frequent that I began to stay away. I got sick of hearing it and was sick of putting him through the verbal abuse.

When I finally got my engagement ring, I began wearing it. One day while visiting my mom and sister at mom's house, mom noticed the ring and asked, "Oh, you got an engagement ring? What pawn shop did he get it from?"

Yes, it had come from a pawn shop but, wow!

The HOPE

I called Ms. Gloria, one of my clients who had been happily married for forty-two years. I told her about all my mother's attacks against John and myself. I asked her how to handle this and what should I do. She told me to calm down and reminded me that she had an appointment the following day so we could have girl talk then.

Ms. Gloria met with me the following morning for her appointment. From there, Ms. Gloria continued to recount the testimony of how her husband, Allen, would walk in and out of jobs in a heartbeat or as soon as someone said something to him that he didn't like; his battles and addictions to drugs and alcohol. She explained how he finally got it together and decided to go back to school and earned a Bachelor's degree in IT while she worked and supported him and their two daughters. How God blessed him with a job in computers and in just six months, he was promoted. How she continued to go to church, without her husband, who would distract her or discourage her from not only going to church but from reading her Bible. Four years of consistent prayer and believing with Christ, her husband saw the Christ in her (1 Peter 3:1), began to go to church also, eventually getting saved and serving in the church. Allen was eventually in the sound financial position of allowing Beverly the blessing of being a stay-at-home wife, mom and grandma for the past thirty-five years. She was very transparent and assured me that the Glory of GOD kept her through it all and how He created a new man and a new marriage right before her eyes. **FORTY-TWO** years later they are still happy and in love; it's **infectious**.

Mrs. Donna, the office manager, stepped in with a very similar testimony about how she and her husband got married while he was still broke and in college. Twenty-eight years later, they're still together and HAPPY. They BOTH talked about the goodness and

Glory of God and how God was with them and their marriages and how they weathered the storms. "There is nothing too hard for GOD," they both assured me.

They advised me, "KEEP FAMILY OUT OF YOUR RELATIONSHIP!" I told them that his mom was very cool, very supportive, that she and I were very close. They again warned, "Keep family **out** of your relationship. When it all boils down to it, blood is thicker than water and that is her son."

They continued to tell me their testimonies and how it related to John and me. They believed GOD and what he could do in and through us; they gave me hope.

I was moved by Ms. Beverly's and Mrs. Donna's love walks, their love for their husbands, families and God. I began to attend their church and eventually ended up joining and becoming a faithful member. I had hope.

CHAPTER 9

The Ex

While dating John, he and Deirdre, Taylor's mom, were in a custody battle. Therefore, he and his mom had a lot to say about her (red flag), "She is crazy. Her own parents don't like her. She loves married men. She moves in with another man every four months dragging Taylor with her," they continually extolled.

They bragged about a time when John, Deirdre and Taylor had gone to her hometown to visit her family in Memphis, TN. He felt she was cheating because she wanted to hang out with her friends for a while, so he left her and eight-month-old Taylor there to find their way back to Dallas.

"I left her, she didn't leave me," he explained with his mom supporting and backing him up.

Taylor and I had a very tight bond. One day after church, we had planned to take Taylor with us on an outing. While John was still serving, I was in the lobby and walked into Deirdre who was holding Taylor. I said hi to Deirdre and immediately, Taylor looked my direction and leaped into my arms. Deirdre said, "Oh, mommy will see you later, Taylor." With her head lying on my shoulder, she waved. She kissed her on the forehead and walked away.

When John was finished, I told him and his mom what had happened and that it seemed Deirdre wasn't too happy about Taylor leaping into my arms and laying her head on my shoulder. They laughed and thought it was funny because they felt, "that's what she get for being bitter," but I felt bad; she had to feel a little dejected.

Deirdre was a single working mother who had just received her doctorate's degree and was preparing to take the bar exam to become a defense attorney. I personally thought she was a doing a good having accomplished this while parenting young Taylor and Amber (her seventeen-year-old from a previous marriage).

She and John would get into shouting matches often when I was present. But when I wasn't around, John would tell me, "Deirdre called me; she is bitter because she still wants me and I'm with you."

Then, I'd talk to Deirdre and she'd say, "John calls me and try to come see me and our daughter. He calls often when you aren't around."

Because we all were members of the same church, I came in contact with Deirdre many times. When I first met her, she had long hair. The next Sunday, she had the exact haircut and curl style that I was wearing.

Other members, including John's mom, began to ask me, "Is Deirdre trying to look like you???"

She began to dress differently also as one member noticed, "She used to be homely, now she has spiced herself up lately."

John told me, "I told you she was crazy. She just wants to be with me. She mad because I left her."

Ms. Brenda added, "I told you she was crazy."

Surely, I knew Deirdre couldn't have wanted John back more than the simple fact of her not wanting John to be with me.

I told John, "This is not about you. She doesn't want you with me. The next thing she will do is buy another car and a house."

John assured me, "No, her Camry is paid for."

Sure enough, Deirdre bought a Lexus, and a house.

CHAPTER 10

Before We Wed

One beautiful Sunday after church, John and I were sitting on the patio playing cards, watching the game and drinking beer. Before I had gotten too comfortable, I left and took my mom a plate because John had just bar-b-cued. While there, she told me she wanted to call and apologize to John for how she had been acting. I told her **no**, because he had been drinking and I suggested that she call another day. Sure enough, by the time I had gotten home, John was on the phone, seemingly upset. My mom had called John after I had just asked her not to.

"Well, you can come to the wedding but after that, I don't want to have anything else to do with you because you are just going to start back talking to me crazy again, then, come back and apologize again. Hello? Hello?" He turned to me and said, "Your mom just hung up on me."

OH MY GOSH, did I get a phone call from my mom? I had taken her cell phone by mistake and by the time I had returned to her house, which was five minutes away, she swung the door open, paused, then shockingly said, "Tori, what happened to your face??? Look Shon, Look at Tori's face." I could feel the numbness on the right side of my face, but I didn't know that there was no movement.

"We're taking you to the hospital!'" They took me straight to the ER. I had Bell's Palsy. One week before my wedding I had lost movement to the right side of my face.

I went back home to John, the man I was about to marry the very next week, and told him that I had Bell's Palsy. I explained to him what it was and how it happens.

John said, "OH, THAT DEVIL IS A LIE," and made a point to make me happy and laugh at ALL COST. Everything we talked about or watched was positive, funny and happy. He would grab, flirt, kiss, hug and hold me every time he looked at me. Hours later, it began to wear off. The next morning, my bottom lip was still numb but my face was completely normal again. Woo, that was a blessing!

Fired: 3 Days before Our Wedding

John had applied to a high-profile company and after the three interviews, criminal background check, pre-employment drug screen and physical; he was finally hired. It was a long process, but it paid handsomely so we were thrilled.

After three days of working and now three days before our wedding, John called Ms. Brenda crying and hysterical. She and I were together doing some last-minute shopping for the wedding. From what I could make of it, John had been let go. I figured that maybe it could've been a trial and he just didn't make the cut. I asked Ms. Brenda if I could speak with him, she passed me the phone. I, first of all, asked him to pull over because he was hysterical, and briefly talked about how David encouraged himself

(1 Samuel 30:6,) that more opportunities are on their way and that I still loved him. Then, I handed the phone back to his mom while we continued to shop. Ms. Brenda began comforting and encouraging John, but I was very curious to know exactly what happened after JUST THREE DAYS. Basically, he was fired from the company for asking the manager for an advance because he had no money for gas to get back home and back to work the next morning. She went on to tell him that God has something better for him and all of that still-attached-umbilical-cord garbage when the bottom line was, WHO asks their employer for gas money after only being employed **three** days?

In my spirit, I knew I was in trouble because that made **no** sense. He could've gone to ANYONE else but an employer of three days. However, I didn't want to burn with lust (1 Cor 7:9) and our wedding was already set in **three** days. Plus, I convinced myself that John could change because *God can change anyone's situation.* And also, as Maya Angelou say, "When you know better, you do better." I thought, *so John may not have been exposed to a lot, but I already have the torch. Eventually when he learns and catches up, I can pass it to him.*

The Marriage

CHAPTER 11

If It Could Go Wrong, IT DID!

The Wedding Day

The night before the wedding, we had rehearsal. Everyone who was part of the wedding was there; his mom and dad, his sisters, cousins, elder cousin Barbara, and a few of my clients, Mrs. Beverly, Mrs. Donna, who were decorating the gazebo and Apostle Roberts. I had no wedding planner, but everyone there was excited about pitching in where they could. John's family was ecstatic and very helpful. His elder cousin, Barbara, was very excited and wanted to help any way possible so we made her an acting wedding coordinator.

The wedding was at the Embassy Suites hotel that had an absolutely amazingly beautiful tropical atrium. There were trees and plants everywhere, marble tables with small candles placed carefully on each one. We had received a blessing with the cost; this was an excellent deal with the cost of having our wedding there and the buffet line setting all included.

I had gotten no sleep as I had worked ALL NIGHT on the wedding (or obituary rather I would discover later) program. My mom called me at 7:00 that morning to inform me that she had just made a peach cobbler and ribs since she figured the family would come to her house after the wedding, instead of mine. *Hmmm, why would they, but ok,* I thought. I asked her if she had gone to pick up the wedding cake and she said, "Not yet."

Mom called me about an hour later and told me that my uncle was at my dad's to pick him up and bring him to Dallas with him, but my dad was high and didn't remember. I called my uncle's cell and asked him to put my dad on the phone. I couldn't understand a word my dad was saying, but I did hear the part about him saying he could not make my wedding because he had some things to do.

John's mom called to tell me that one of my bridesmaids, her niece, could not make the flight. With everything wrong that was happening, Veronica continued to keep me calm and John called often telling me not to stress and to say something funny.

Mom called around noon to tell me that she was not going to have time to pick up the wedding cake because she had been cooking all morning. About thirty minutes later, she called back to tell me to stop what I was doing to go and pick it up. I told her that I was on my way to the church and that I was not going to worry about it.

She goes off, "YOU ARE NOT GONNA HAVE A CAKE? WHAT WEDDING DO YOU KNOW OF THAT DON'T HAVE A WEDDING CAKE? SO Y'ALL JUST GONNA HAVE THE CAKE THAT HIS MAMA MADE???"

She continued yelling at me until I finally told her that I had to get off the phone because I was already stressed. It was already 12:50 p.m. and the wedding started at 1:00 p.m.

While driving to the church and my sister, who should've already been there, called, "Tori, mom told me to go get your cake!"

Frustrated, I told her, "No! Go straight to the church, we're already late! We have no time for anything else!"

John called wondering where I was, but tells me to calm down and everything was going to be alright. He cracked a few more jokes to make me laugh.

A Beautiful Disaster

I made it to the church at 1:15 p.m. The wedding was supposed to start at 1:00 p.m. I immediately told them to start while I ran to the hotel restroom to get dressed. I began dressing into my Cinderella dress with pearls surrounding the front upper torso, with the back in the shape of a corset tying down, tiara, cancan slip, clear shoes. Different family members that were coming to use the restroom saw me and began to help, expressing their excitement or simply encouraging me. By this time, there was about ten of my family and friends in the restroom when someone asked if I wanted my mom to come in and help; I said, no. The restroom had become completely silent, but I could only think of the stress she had been putting me through all morning up until half hour prior: calling, complaining and yelling. All I needed was to get through the next few hours without Bell's Palsy.

Again, I had no wedding coordinator, so everyone that came to the wedding rehearsal the night before already had decided where they were going to sit. My mother and her friend came to the hotel, but they would not get out of the car. I had told his older cousin, Barbara, where I wanted my mom and family to sit. Maybe it was a bit much for her or she had forgotten because I later learned that when my mom was escorted in, all the seats were taken, therefore leaving her standing and holding onto my nephew's arm. In front of everyone looking on, she finally asked if my cousin would give up his seat for her to sit down. Because I was in the back, I had no knowledge of this; I thought everything was going as planned.

When my grandfather had come to the back to see me, I asked if he would walk me down the aisle since I had just found out a few hours prior that my dad was too high to remember this important day of my life and told me that he "had things to do." My grandfather had been having problems with his leg and did not feel comfortable walking me down, so I was prepared to walk alone. Then, here comes my brother smiling, dressed in a black suit, white shirt, black and white striped tie, silver cuff links and black shoes. I asked him if he'd escort me and surprised, he said, "My little sis wants me to walk her down the aisle? SURE!" I was SO EXCITED! I was so happy that someone from my side of the family was back there and happy that I was happy. Whatever he thought of my husband-to-be or if I was making the biggest mistake of my life, he never said it. He smiled at me and put his elbow out for me to take it. I guess his big brother instincts kicked in and he may have felt that I was on the brink of breaking down.

As we began to walk, he joyfully said, "Tori, this is your day, this is your day, be happy!"

Everything was going great. My brother made jokes as we walked. Then, we were close enough to see my husband-to-be, who almost fell off the stage trying to watch me come down the aisle, with the BIGGEST grin on his face. My brother even noticed it and made a joke.

John and I were finally face-to-face before my brother gave me away. Everyone's taking pictures and smiling. John stood there, handsome in a white tux with black trimmings, white tux shirt, silver cuff links, black bow tie and black patent leather shoes. His face was blood shot red with tears streaming and he was cheesing so hard. He looked fantastic. He was happy and I was happy (as if he were gainfully employed). Our guests were happy. Well, most of them.

When my brother gave me away, John whispered in my ear, "You look beautiful," as I took his arm to walk up the stairs onto the stage before the pastor.

Standing next to me was my maid of honor, Veronica, and standing next to him was his Uncle Jeff. My bridesmaids: two of his sisters and my angry sister. His cousin, and both of my ecstatic younger brothers, stood in all black with white flowers and corsages on the stage behind the gazebo.

My Apostle and god-father was the officiate. When we walked into the gazebo where he was standing with the best man and my maid of honor, he looked me in the eyes and whispered, "Are you alright?"

Smiling, I answered, "Yes."

He was cracking jokes and keeping the wedding in a positive and upbeat manner. Because he was there the night before, he was aware of what was going on between my mom and me.

When it came time for the lighting of the unity candle, John's mom came into the gazebo; my mom didn't. She sat and watched. I motioned her to come up, but she just sat there. Keeping a smile on my face while my heart had just sank into my stomach from embarrassment, I looked around thinking, *who's going to light the unity candle from my side of the family? Surely, this is not happening.* Yes, mom had told me to get someone else to do it because she wanted no parts of the wedding, but I guess I thought that she'd change her mind. Once again, my hero, my brother, immediately came up in her place, smiling. I let out a sigh of relief. I could breathe again.

When it came time for us to say our vows, Apostle handed me the microphone, "Do you have something that you would like to say to him?"

Crying, I said yes, then looked at John, "Thank you for keeping me calm with everything that was happening this morning. I love you and you **know** that I need you."

John wiped away his tears. I handed the microphone back to the Apostle and I began to repeat my vows.

When the ceremony was over, John and I stood near the reception entry where everyone was to come and congratulate us. The VERY FIRST PERSON to hug us was his mother. She walked right up to me with the biggest grin and open arms. She then pointed to her famous homemade German Chocolate Cake that she made for the groom's cake. After we hugged, she stood with us to greet and hug our guests. Next to congratulate us were my beloved grandmother and grandfather; then the rest of our family and friends. Everyone hugged and congratulated us, everyone but my mom and my sister.

People pretended not to notice that the wedding didn't have a wedding cake and I, the Bride, didn't have her mother. My mother and sister were on the side of the elevator mad, upset and complaining to the other members of my family standing with them.

My husband, my wedding party (except my sister) and I were taking pictures. My aunt came and hugged me, letting me know that she was about to leave. I looked around; **my family was gone** except my grandparents, my brother and my sister-in-law.

Guests came to me after the wedding and asked why was my mom crying and why did she leave; why didn't my sister smile while walking down the aisle or took any pictures with the wedding party? Needless to say, we left after the reception got started. I couldn't take it anymore.

The RECEPTION: ALL TWO OF US

At home, there was Veronica, Cameron, John and me. I called my mom to find out if anyone was still there, so that Cameron could catch a ride back to Oklahoma. In the background, there was a party happening. My family had actually left my wedding and went to my mom's house. Devastated? Yes.

Shocked? No. My mom is not only the baby of her family, but she is her mom's miracle baby because she came seven years after her tubes were tied.

Mom has always been the life of the party. My grandma is the baby of her siblings, so she was also the life of the party also. Every holiday would either be at my grandparent's house or our house. But either way, my mom was always the life of the party.

CHAPTER 12

I Married My Best Friend

John was my best friend. Whether we took a trip out on the town or simply stayed at home, we could always manage to entertain each other. He and I did everything together. We enjoyed each other immensely. John's comedic proclivities and my witty sense of humor always guaranteed entertainment. John was more of the extrovert, who didn't know a stranger, while I was more of the introvert that had to warm up to you. We laughed a lot and we could find the humor in just about anything. We knew each other so well that we knew which type of situation would warrant a particular reaction. All of this led to us feeding off of each other no matter the situation. Even at a church marriage retreat, people left knowing who we were. Having fun with each other gave us more joy than having fun with others. Sometimes he could go a little too far, but I knew he was trying to be funny. To this day, people still remember us as one of the funniest couples they had ever met.

We could have a huge argument and he would still do something to make me laugh. For example, one day we had an argument and I went downstairs and laid on the living room couch.

About thirty minutes later, he came storming down the steps into the room yelling, "TORI, HOW LONG ARE YOU GOING TO STAY MAD? I'M SICK OF THIS ATTITUDE AND DO YOU THINK…"

I turned over, cutting him off and began yelling back, "WELL, YOU SHOULD HAVE..."

Then, I couldn't talk; I paused and honed in on what he had on. This six feet two inches 280 pound football-built man was standing there with my skintight, white laced, short party dress on with no socks or shoes. I stared at him for a second, and he stared back looking both serious and angry. I could no longer hold it in; I burst into laughter.

Then there was a time when I was pregnant, and my client Vickie, who taught Jazzercise, had called to check on my pregnancy. She (49) and John (34) began to go back-and-forth about what was real exercise, stamina and how he could do such a better job at teaching her class that they would want to replace her with him. Suddenly, she challenged him to come to the class that she was teaching that evening. Sad to say, we went and after twenty minutes, he fell out. I was laughing because I was seven months pregnant and I was still able to keep up.

When that session was over, she passed John and I who were sitting in the back of the room, and said, "I'll be right back; I'm going to change shirts for my second session."

When she was well out of ear shot, John muttered, "Tori, come on!"

I asked, "What, why?"

He grabbed my things beckoning for me, "HURRY UP! Hurry before she comes back. LET'S GO!"

He then grabbed my arm with one hand and placed his other hand on my back politely rushing me out of the chair, so we could scurry out of the door. In that short time of her just changing shirts, we were gone. He yelled, "Vickie's crazy for thinking people can do all that. That's too much!"

Cracking up, I said, "John, we were the youngest people in there and I'm seven months pregnant. You are the only one in that packed class that fell out onto the ground."

There was another time when our neighbors, a block over, were having a big party outside by their pool.

John said, "I need a drink. Let's go crash that party, baby!"

I disagreed so John said, "Well, I'm just going to find where the country and western music is coming from."

Next thing I knew, John came back with four beers, "C'mon baby, they told me to come get my wife!"

We were so close and our love was so passionate that John and I held hands every time we made love. We snuggled **every** single night. Many nights we would talk until day light. I often laid my head on his chest while he would rub my hair. We'd read the Bible together. We loved watching movies. We went to church together. We invited couples over once a month. We loved to do family things with Cameron, Taylor and Ms. Brenda. We just loved being together.

I never felt like I had to compete for his love. I had a fantastic relationship with his mom and his daughter. I loved the way John loved me. There was not much that we did not do together. He was my heart and I knew I was his.

External influences internally

On the other hand, I received a phone call regarding my marriage to John, DAILY.

"Where is John working this week? Is he bringing any income in? Why are you two pretending to be happy? Everyone can see right through it. How happy can you be when he won't keep a job and you're stuck with all the bills? You brag about what a great father he is to Taylor, but she is ALWAYS with you! You don't mind carrying him? That's going to get old soon. God is not going to bless you all because you didn't listen to your mother. I told you not to marry him, now look at you. No one is happy for you. God won't take responsibility for something that He didn't put together..."

This was EVERY SINGLE DAY!

So, I finally asked, "Mom, do you suggest I divorce my husband?" I asked.

"I don't know what you should do. I'm just letting you know what you've done and God is not going to bless it."

CHAPTER 13

The First Argument

After being married for nearly a month and a half, John and I met up at a restaurant for lunch one afternoon to come up with a plan for spending his insurance settlement wisely. I began jotting down all of our expenses and plans to get John current on the child support and car note the he was behind on. I knew when I married John that he was behind in child support and his car note, but I was also aware of this upcoming settlement. We didn't have to worry about his cell phone being cut off anymore because I put him on my plan. John was approximately $3,500 behind in child support and approximately $2,500 behind on his car note. I told him to pay them both up, which would make him current, but John didn't think it was a wise decision.

"Why?" I asked.

He answered, "Because Apostle tells us not to pay all our bills up when we come into money." Dumb-founded, I asked, "He actually got up on the pulpit in front of thousands of members and said, 'Don't pay your bills up if you come into money?'"

"Yes," he answered, "because we will always have bills so we need to invest and…"

"Oh, okay. Sweetie, that's not what he meant. Surely he meant not to go and pay cash for a house or car then have nothing to maintain those things, your life or your family thereafter. I'm sure he was advising us to build our credit, buy property or invest; do something productive with the money and let it work for itself. Plus, you are BEHIND in your expenses so clearly that wouldn't apply to you. You have to be caught up, babe," I added.

Hoping John understood what the Apostle meant, I continued to go down the list and what it cost to run our household. We agreed to split the current month's mortgage, taxes, homeowner's insurance, electricity, water, gas and groceries down the middle. He agreed and handed me the money right then.

Okay, I told John, that after the money for this month, getting current on his child support and his car, this will leave him with nearly $2,000 to buy some things that he NEEDED and put the rest into a savings account. I felt this could hold him while he job searched. I also asked him did he want to send some money to the Deirdre to help with some of Taylor's daycare expenses.

He responded, "NO, LET HER BOYFRIEND PAY IT!"

What happened to the money?

He gave me money for the bills at our house for that month, we ate steak and lobster, took his niece school shopping and bought a couple of things for the house. It felt good for the simple fact that I was able to show him that when you take care of your responsibilities first, you are able to reward yourself and have money in savings. I thought this was the perfect opportunity to illustrate how you can live when you have money.

I felt good about our discussion, plans and agreement. At least, I *thought* it was ours. Later, I found that he was just playing, he had to have had his fingers crossed behind his back. He pretended to be involved when actually, he knew, that money was already spent in his head.

Three weeks later, I met with Deirdre to take Taylor back. I asked her, "Is everything okay now? Is John caught up?"

Confused she answered, "Caught up? I've only gotten $300."

Once again, I saw that dark cloud hover the earth, but, I did not react in front of her, simply saying, "Oh, okay."

Here we go!

That forty-five minute drive home turned into twenty minutes. I believe I came around the corner on two wheels. I walked into the door where John was sitting on the couch watching the game.

I calmly asked, "John how much money do you have left?"

John, with a confused look, uttered, "Huh?"

"You had $2,000 left. I know you bought a couple of things for the house, for yourself, for your niece and we went out to eat a few times. How much money do you have left?"

John went back over everything I had just mentioned and added the child support and the truck note, then said, "I spent it all on you all."

Trying to remain calm, I asked, "John, just two weeks ago, you received a $9,900 settlement, and you and I sat at the restaurant and wrote out a plan on how to get you caught up. Did you follow that plan?"

"Yes," he answered.

"Okay," I asked, "Why is Deirdre claiming that you only gave her $300?"

THE DIVORCE

To make a long story short, it boiled down to the fact that in a mere two weeks, John had blown nearly $7,000. John had only paid $300 on the $3,500 that he owed for child support. So, I should expect to continue to receive letters from the Attorney General's office and attitudes from Taylor's mom. And the $520 of the $2,500 that he owed for the car meant that any day now, they would find out where John lived and would come to Frisco with that big truck alerting neighbors that someone in this house was irresponsible.

I could not believe it. This basically meant that John had lied to me before we walked out the door because he knew full well that he was not going to follow that plan.

CHAPTER 14

Power: Given or Taken

The last guy I dated had NO drama from his daughter, Jamie's, mom. One day he called, not knowing that I had gotten married. We caught up, then I asked him how he had avoided the drama. During the two years we dated, I never, EVER heard a foul word come out of his mouth about his daughter, Jamie's mother. He never seemed stressed regarding not being able to spend time with her, nor did she ever call cursing him out.

He answered, "I had learned from other men who did NOT have BABY MAMA DRAMA. First of all, that's MY daughter, too, that she takes care of on a FULL-TIME BASIS. Secondly, Jamie's mom will always make sure that Jamie is taken care of, but I **want** to be a part of that. She is MY daughter and I have just as much rights and RESPONSIBILITIES as her mother does. She has never had to put me on child support because once we realized that relationship wasn't going to work, we had to figure the best way we could both get along and co-parent for the health, well-being and stability for our daughter. More than anything, a man doesn't need anyone to tell him to be responsible. I don't **want** ANYONE, either a judge or district attorney to **make me** take care of what's **mine**. If I allow that to happen, then the judge now has a part in my daughter's life and how I visit, pay and parent her. I refuse to give anyone that much power or control over me. If Jamie's mom is not stressed, then she can better parent my daughter. She does not, and WILL NOT, have to ask me for money because Jamie needs pampers, shoes and clothes. Originally, we agreed on a certain amount for me to pay every month but I give her that and pay for daycare, take her to gymnastics practices and some doctor appointments. I get Jamie for the weekend, every other weekend and sometimes, I allow her sister to come with her if she's not with her dad the weekend that I get Jamie."

He continued, "I don't get it when men say they don't support their own child because the mother can afford it, they are mad at her or he doesn't want the child's mother to buy herself something with it. If the child is not living in good condition with heat, water, a roof over their heads, proper clothes and shoes, than the dad needs to take custody, but if that child is being provided for and you've moved on, SO WHAT!

Now on the other hand, there are some mothers that have not moved on, so they 'beat the daddy with the baby,' by not letting him see the child and games like that. In that case, he would **have to** get a judge involved because she has NO right to use their child to **control** him. Just because they could not make it as a couple, it doesn't mean they can't make it as great co-parents.

In the beginning, Jamie's mother had a time when she would demand answers, 'Where are you going? Who are you with? Are you putting someone over your child?' When they play games, they're saying, 'I still love and want you,' which she admitted. But when she stopped, I knew she had moved on and couldn't care less what I was doing as long as I am a great dad to Jamie."

CHAPTER 15

Fired or Quit

I knew my family and John's oldest sister, Kelly, were not happy about our union. John was deemed a loser, a joke. And Kelly often found a way to make a mockery of him in front of any and every one. In fact, when I first met her, she looked at me and said, "Don't get pregnant by him." Now he was my husband, and I did not care what others thought of him. I knew John had potential once he had opportunity or exposure to something greater. I knew I already had material goods, so that part John did not have to worry about. I was there for him, to see him accomplish his dream of becoming a physical therapist. He was my husband and to me, there was nothing that he could not become and I was going to support him in any way I could. I was fine with John working part-time at UPS while he was in school. I believed in him and I was willing to pay all the bills including his car payment, child support or whatever. We were going to shock everyone that wrote him off, that called him stupid, and me.

Okay, Plan B

After the first semester, John quit school because he said it wasn't for him. Also, John was no longer employed at UPS. He said he walked off because he didn't like the way they had talked to him.

John and I had come up with a plan to start his own catering business. Stylists can often times be in a salon working all day and not get a chance to eat or go out to eat. So, I suggested to John to cater to salons while he continued to get a pyramid business that sold juice off the ground. I joined the business with John for support.

I believed in John, so I invested in his juice business and his catering business by buying everything that he would need to get it going. John's mom was a great cook and John was able to get pointers from her while he went to the community college.

CHAPTER 16

The UNDERSTANDING

Whenever John and I would have a disagreement, it seemed Deirdre suddenly appeared in the picture. John always let me know that Deirdre called him complaining, needing something for Taylor, or asking why John married me and what's going on with us? John informed me that Deirdre was disappointed for not being told about the upcoming wedding, and Taylor gaining a new stepmom. He told me that she also wanted to know why he married me and not her and told him that he would never love me the way he loved her.

One day, Taylor came over, and as soon as she walked in the door, she jumped into my arms and said, "T.T., my mommy said I have ONLY ONE MOMMY AND ONE DADDY!"

I looked over at John and he shook his head. It seemed to be getting worse with Taylor feeling she had to choose between T.T. and mommy. Why does she keep sending her over here with messages? I never thought she would be a problem because she had already been in a live-in relationship with him, so she knew the bullet she had dodged. So, what's the problem?

That evening, on my way to work, I called Deirdre. I thought it would be reasonable to clear the air and answer any questions or concerns that she may have about me, especially now that I would be a part of Taylor's life.

She answered, "Hello?"

I responded, "Hi, Deirdre, this is Tori. How are you? I'm fine and you? I'm fine. I'm calling because I spoke with John and he mentioned that you were a bit upset about our not meeting before the wedding and you were upset that he didn't tell you."

Calm, but with a slight defensive attitude, she responded, "Well, I feel that he should have told me first that he was getting married. He never told me anything. I found out by seeing the wedding ring on his finger when he brought Taylor back the weekend you two got married. He should have told me also because I have his daughter. I should have been the first to know; I felt disrespected."

I retorted, "Deirdre, I apologize that you feel disrespected but John and his mom both had their reasons *(she is crazy)* for not informing you, besides the fact that he doesn't need your blessing or permission."

With an attitude, she said, "Well, I thought that we should have gotten a chance to get know each other, so we all could be on the same page. And you and John would know what I expect from you two because I WILL WHOOP SOMEBODY ABOUT MY DAUGHTER!"

I didn't respond; I was warned that she "was crazy."

I guess remembering the reason that John told her that he loved me, "...because she is classy," she continued, "Tori?"

I replied, "Yes?"

"I am a very educated woman; I have a Doctorate's degree," she added.

"Great, so there's no reason that we cannot all get along, especially for Taylor's sake," I commented, "Do you have any questions for me?"

"Well, I just think we should all be on the same page," she added.

"I agree and I will talk with John and his mom tonight, that way you don't have to call him upset or inquiring about his reasons for marrying me," I said.

"That's not me. He is the one that calls telling me the reason that he married you because you were 'classy' and trying to make me jealous. He is the one who said he would never love you like he loved me; he calls me saying all that. My biggest complaint was that he is over there helping you with all your bills but not helping me with Taylor until Ms. Brenda told me that you are carrying the load. He tried to marry me a year ago and came to me with one of his mom's old rings talking about moving me in with them. I told him, 'No!'

I know they be calling me 'crazy,' but I'm not crazy. I just want John to respect me," she said.

"You are right. And you should be respected if for no other reason, for you being Taylor's mother. Okay, like I said, I will speak with them tonight. As you may already know, Taylor and I have a very good relationship and I would never do anything to hurt her nor would I allow anyone to hurt her. She is a good kid and I think you've done an amazing job with her."

"Thank you," she said.

"Have a good day," I said and ended the call.

CHAPTER 17

IN FRONT OF OUR CHILDREN AND FRIENDS!

John and I had been married a year now. He had quit or been fired from at least eleven jobs. This time he claimed he *had* quit his job at the wireless company, so this particular morning, he was supposed to be on an interview in Keller, TX. He called after the interview to tell me he was going to stop by Jeremy and Angela's house before making the hour drive back home. Jeremy and John were both part of the usher ministry at the church. He and his wife, Angela, were **finally** expecting their first child. In addition, they owned a beautiful home in South Lake, TX. That afternoon, John called to let me know that he had gone to the gas station for water because he was "so thirsty," and he ran into Deirdre and Taylor. (Red flag) John would never, ever stop at a gas station to buy water before getting to Jeremy's house, especially a gas station that's just five minutes away. Jeremy and Angela shopped at Sam's, so their pantry **stayed** full of goodies and drinks. So, I began to question over and over --why, how, what had he been doing that would cause such a thirst to where he could not wait until he had gotten to Jeremy's house; and why didn't he call before he drove that direction to find that Jeremy was not home?

I knew my husband and I did not buy the story nor could I let it go. So, I called Deirdre.

"Hi, Deirdre, how are you? Did you all have a safe vacation? Blah, blah, blah." I continued, "Great, and John told me that he ran into you at the Conoco?"

Shocked, she answered, "Gas station? No, no, John was at my apartment."

She confirmed what I already knew. I knew John did not see her at a gas station but in fact, he had gone to her apartment, but I had to hear it.

"At your apartment?" I asked.

"Yes, I had an anonymous call on my home phone, then five minutes later, he was knocking at my door."

I could not finish my client's hair fast enough. I don't remember her giving me cash or running her credit card, if I did. I jumped in the car and called his mom and told her everything. She told me to calm down because I had become very emotional as I drove home.

I walked in the door yelling, "What the HELL IS WRONG WITH YOU, JOHN!!" (I'm not a cusser and for me to go there, it was totally out of character but I had had it).

He came down the steps explaining the **same story** that he had rehearsed previously, "Tori, I was thirsty so I stopped at the..."

OH MY GOSH, I could not hear anything else. If I didn't believe it the first twenty times, surely he'd change something about the story. So, every time he gave me this one, it further infuriated me.

I called Deirdre on my cell and put her on speaker. She answered and John started talking, "Deirdre, didn't I see you at the gas station?"

Deirdre answered, "John, don't sit there and lie. You know you didn't see me at a gas station. You were here at my apartment eating off Taylor's plate until I asked you, 'Do your wife know that you are here?'"

"YOU ARE A LIE, YOU ARE LYING!!! DEIRDRE, WHY ARE YOU TRYING TO CAUSE PROBLEMS?" John retorted yelling.

John and Deirdre began a shouting match, then she finally said, "You were in here. DO YOU WANT ME TO PUT YOUR DAUGHTER ON THIS PHONE?"

I ended the charade by cutting in saying, "Deirdre, thank you and have a nice evening."

I couldn't understand why John couldn't just simply tell the truth, "You were in the area, you figured Deirdre and Taylor were home from their vacation and you decided to stop by. I would not have been happy, but at least I would have had to respect your honesty. But to lie, not only lie, but to give me a story that was completely unbelievable. You even said yourself, 'I don't know why nobody believes me!' That tells me that your mom called you after she hung up with me, and she did not buy that story either. That is not your character, John, we know you!"

I put the phone down, walked upstairs and went to bed sleeping only on the seam.

The next day, we were invited to come hang out, as usual, at Jeremy and Angela's house. We did our married couple's talk as usual; but, this time was different. John and I were not joking, flirting, nor playing around. They asked what was wrong and John began to explain that same story, "Well, I was thirsty…"

Immediately I went from 0 to 10 in sixty seconds, only seeing red, as the dark cloud began to hover the earth!

After John finished, everyone sat in silence. Then, Jeremy finally said, "C'mon, John!"

I, remaining calm, began telling them about the phone call with Deirdre. John continued with the story and eventually he and I started arguing. That moment came when John said, "You sound stupid!"

UH-OH!

I don't remember feeling my heart beating. I only felt steam leaving my ears and head only seeing the words "You" and "Stupid." Because Angela was pregnant, I suggested that we leave. John called Taylor and Cameron and we jumped in the car, now arguing quietly. Angela and Jeremy walked us outside, careful not to get involved.

Finally, I told him that I was dropping him off at his mom's house, "Hurry up, because I'm getting ready to drop you off at your mom's house. In fact, get out! I'm driving because this is my car; I bought this car!"

He began to laugh and became very sarcastic.

Angrily, I demanded, "Get out, get out, get out of the car, now!"

THE DIVORCE

I got out of the passenger side of the car, walked around to the driver's side and stood in front of him quietly demanding, "John get out of the car. John, get your punk a** out of the car!"

John quietly retorted, "B*tch, get your a** in the car."

I reacted, "B*TCH???" In that split second, *all I could see were: the nights I stayed up taking care of Taylor when she was sick or had ear infections; the long forty-five minute drives to pick her up from school; the month of July where I kept Taylor with me so that she could stay with us the entire month; the shopping for Taylor because she had NO clothes; taking Taylor to work with me and to the rent house; the bills that John couldn't pay, the bills that John **caused** that he couldn't pay; the baby mama drama; the child support that I PAID, the truck note that I PAID, the truck we were arguing in, that I BOUGHT, and the word that came to his mind was, "B*TCH!!!"* I went into a full rage and began hitting him.

We began to scuffle, then John put me in some kind of self-defense hold and slammed my body and face into the side of the truck. As John had me pinned against the door and window, I saw the look in the shocked three-year-olds Taylors' eyes. You could see the fear. I could not see Cameron who was sitting in the back on the passenger side. Afterwards, John yanked me back off the car, he and I were facing the same direction against each other, except he was six feet two inches 280 pounds and I was five feet five inches 145 pounds. Rage + body slam = psychopathy. John was no longer my husband, and we were no longer in front of church members (one who was eight months pregnant) and our children. John was now a crazed lunatic that just slammed me into a car. He was now my enemy. I tried to wiggle my way out of the hold that he had me in while kicking his shins, ankles and feet as a mad woman who was in a full-blown, infuriated rage.

In the midst of out tussle, Jeremy approached us very calmly and said, "John, John, let me get your wife."

As soon as I heard Jeremy, I immediately calmed completely down. I had a great deal of respect for Jeremy as a friend, a minister and a well-balanced, wise man. He and Angela were like brother and sister to us. They were our confidantes and mentors. We loved them and they loved us. They even fronted us the money for us to go on a cruise with them (John never repaid his half). Jeremy and John had both taken self-defense classes once upon a time, so when Jeremy, about five feet nine inches, grabbed my arms, they both turned me into some type of swing out and stand position, where my arms were still folded behind my back, all while still bracing themselves for the worse.

Jeremy, who had me by both arms, called my name, "Tori, Tori?"

I wouldn't answer; I couldn't answer. A tear fell as I could not find a way to look up at him. Realizing that I had completely come into embarrassment, Jeremy sympathetically let me go. I walked around John, climbed into the driver's seat and shut the door while continually wiping tears from my eyes with my head down. I was so embarrassed. John and I had made a complete fool of ourselves in front of our children and our friends.

I finally got the courage to look at Angela, who by this time, was nervously smacking on the crumbs in the bag of Cheetos that she had just finished.

I mouthed to her, "I'm sorry," as I could no longer hold back the tears. They were in full flow. She put her hand up to her ear in phone position and said, "That's okay, call me," while she continued to stick her hand in the bag finding only cheese to eat off of her fingers.

John got in the car and I drove off; both of us wiping tears, no one saying anything. Jeremy called twice to check on us. Twenty-five minutes later, we arrived at his mother's, 11:45 p.m.

I parked and whispered, "Get out!"

He wouldn't move.

I got out of the car and unbuckled frightened Taylor out of her car seat and held her while walking her through her grandmother's door. The door was unlocked because Cameron had jumped out and gone to the restroom. Taylor walked into the bedroom with her grandma while I attempted to call a cab because John had taken the keys. John tried to snatch the phonebook out of my hand and we began to quietly wrestle over it.

John's mother came out and yelled, "WHAT'S GOING ON!" as she attempted to find the light switch.

Finally, she found the light and asked again, "What's going on in here?" Then it happened, the unthinkable:

"SHE HIT ME!!!" John cried aloud as he pointed at me.

"HE CALLED ME A B*TCH!!!" I cried pointing back.

"YOU HIT ME, TORI!!!" he cried.

"YOU CALLED ME OUT OF MY NAME, JOHN, ME!" I answered still in shock.

At that very moment, John and I were 2 three-year-olds crying, pointing and telling on each other.

Ms. Brenda said, "Wait a minute, you two sit down; we are not going to let the devil come in."

She began to pray while John and I sat there balling our eyes out. As she prayed, she grabbed John's hand and my hand and placed them together causing us to hold hands. By the time she finished praying, we were hugging, crying and apologizing.

CHAPTER 18

The Arrest

One month later, the afternoon of June 25, my day at work was going great; until I saw Deirdre's number on my cell. At the moment, I had two clients under the dryer, so I stepped out into the hallway of the building.

I answered and Deirdre began, "Tori, I want to let you know that John was over here because the last time y'all called, he tried to put it on me, so I'm letting you know he was over here."

"Deirdre, did he say why he was there?" I asked.

This day was a Wednesday and besides training, this was not a visitation day.

Deirdre began to tell me, "He was just trying to push up on me."

"What does that mean?" I asked.

She answered, "When I opened the door, he grabbed my arm and was trying to hug and kiss on me. I finally got him to stop and told him if he ever did that again, that I was going to call his wife. I called you anyway because I know how he is and how he has been telling you and his mom that I have been calling him trying to get back with him."

I tried to make sense of why my husband was not in training as he got up and got dressed and told me that's where he was going.

Knowing the answer, but hoping for any logical reason as to why John was at Deirdre's, I asked, "Deirdre, where is Taylor?"

She answered, "Tori, you know that Taylor is in daycare and I don't pick her up for another hour."

In efforts to remain professional, I walked as fast as I could, in heels, to my car and called John."

"Hello," John answered.

"JOHN, WHAT THE H*LL WERE YOU DOING AT DEIRDRE'S?" I asked very pissed.

"What are you talking about? You know she be lying. You know she is crazy. I ain't got time for this; I'm back in training," he replied, then he hung up in my face.

In disbelief, I thought, *not only did he just lie to me, but he hung up in my face!*

I called back ten times but John would not answer. I finished working and headed home two hours later.

I got home still in heels and still on 10, "John, I told you to get out!"

John sat there watching TV.

"JOHN, GET OUT! This is not a game. I'm sick of you and your woman. You guys need to be together since every time you and I have an argument, she magically appears and I'm sick of you, SO GET OUT!" I demanded.

"I'm not going anywhere," he responded, "YOU GET OUT! I'M SICK OF YOU, TOO."

Somehow, the more he talked, he began to get angry for real and began to yell, scream and call me stupid. By the time I reached the top of the steps, I began dropping the bags he had packed over the banister. Suddenly, he turned red and began to charge up the steps at full speed, while I continued to throw his things over. John reached the top step and pushed me into the room onto the bed by my face. We wrestled on the bed, so I began kicking him to get him off me and to make sure I blocked him from hitting me. It worked; he got off of me.

I grabbed my cell and called 911, "Hello, operator, will you please send the police out here? My husband and I are fighting and I just need you to send someone out to be here while he get his stuff to leave."

While waiting on the police, I changed out of my work clothes and heels, into a jumper outfit and tennis shoes.

When the police arrived, John ran outside crying, "Look what she did; look what she did. She scratched me. I got scratches on my neck!"

The second police officer, a woman, arrived and pulled me to the side. She asked what happened and who hit first. I told her that he ran up the stairs and pushed me into our room by my face. She asked had anything like this happened before and I told her about to the incident at Jeremy's house when I found out he had been over Deirdre's. **I KNEW** John was going to do whatever he had to do to save himself and sure enough, he DID.

Soon, the two officers and the sergeant came together. What happened next was shocking; she began to read me my rights and place handcuffs on my wrists. As she walked me to the car, I passed John who began to cry hysterically falling to his knees.

I could not understand why I was being arrested, so the officer asked did I want to write a statement about what happened. I thought about it but declined. After all, I loved him.

I went through the whole process of being fingerprinted, pictured and everything being booked entails. It was around 11:30 p.m. when they finished processing me.

They gave me my one phone call, so I called Apostle Roberts, "Apostle, John and I had a fight and they took me to jail."

"WHAT?" he yelled.

I calmly continued, "I've never been to jail before, so I ask for your prayers because I have no idea what to expect."

He prayed for me, but I could hear sorrow in his voice.

After we hung up, they walked me around a corner and had me to change into an orange jail suit then to an empty room with four concrete, thin bunk beds on one wall and two concrete beds along the other. Each bed was fitted with a thin piece of cushion and no pillow. There were no walls or clocks, just a concrete room with a thin blanket.

It was so cold, so cold. I pushed the intercom requesting another blanket.

The bailiff yelled back, "NO!" but it sounded like he was communicating, "THIS IS NOT A HOTEL, YOU ARE IN JAIL!!!"

Between being cold and replaying what happened, I couldn't sleep as I tried to understand how why my own husband allowed me to go to jail, *after* he ran up the stairs and pushed me into a room by my face. I couldn't believe it. I tried to make sense of it and came to the fact that John had been arrested before and had

THE DIVORCE

been to court a few times, so it was probably a good thing because they may have kept him a while. (My mom was right, I had become sick in my own head).

They had a small common area between the four cells in the unit that I was in. It had a concrete table, bench and a phone. The cell doors opening for breakfast where they brought hard donuts, cinnamon rolls, and Danish. I was excited to get to that phone, so I pressed the intercom and asked if I could use it. The bailiff informed me that my husband had been there all morning on a quest to get me out, so I had to call someone who could call him. Sad part, it had to be a landline and everyone I would be willing to call had cell phones. But the only three people who had landlines were the very ones I DID NOT want to find out; my mom and her two sisters. I would not, could not, call my mom, although I knew eventually that she'd find out, so I called my Aunt Joyce whose husband Al called John for me. When I called Uncle Al back, he informed that John was trying to come up with bail money and had begged for officers to not transfer me to the county jail as planned. I told Uncle Al to tell John that when I left work upset the night before, I had forgot and left my money in the drawer and since John had the key to my suite, he could go and get it. But by then, John's mother loaned it to him. Even still, it was a process and a lot of leg work and driving.

I called Uncle Al (RIP) so many times, (the bill came to $147) but each time he was patient. He held my hand through that phone until I was finally released. I was so grateful.

When they released me, I had ONE hour to get home because of my 5 o'clock standing hair appointment, so I began walking. John drove up in my car about ten minutes later from the county. I got in with no words.

He asked, "How does it feel to go to jail?"

I had no words. When he drove into the garage, I jumped out and ran upstairs to get ready for work. John grabbed his bags and left.

Later, I received phone calls from guys asking, why was I calling through the night but not saying anything? I also received a phone call from my mom and sis. Of course, they weren't happy.

Two days later, John came over and asked if we could talk.

I broke down, "I cannot believe you let them take me to jail!"

"You were throwing my stuff!" he responded.

"John, you knew that you started this and you let me spend the night in jail," I cried.

Eventually, he apologized, "I'm sorry. You had never been to jail and I knew it would be easier to bond you back out. Plus, in my line of work, I can't have Domestic Violence on my record."

We talked more, apologized, cried, made love then went to his family reunion.

CHAPTER 19

No More Excuses

My tenants in my rent house had skipped out and left the place a nasty **mess**. There were maggots in dirty dishes, gum in the carpet, holes in walls, dog feces, and tracks in the yard from the U-Haul truck. There was SO MUCH TO DO. My newly built 2400 sq. ft. home in a nice middle class neighborhood was left in a mess. And it was up to me to paint, shampoo carpet, snake toilets, clean tubs and chase a family of rats out of the garage – all by myself. Ms. Brenda, my mom, my sister had come and helped with a project and I was grateful, but there was still so much to do.

Jeremy and Angela were excited for their baby shower that was only three days away. I worked at the shop that morning. (It was July, John's month to keep Taylor, so of course, she was with me). Taylor and I would go clean the rent house in the evenings. Angela begged me to take a break and come to the baby shower.

John was already there. After I had worked at the salon that morning, Taylor and I then headed straight for the rent house. John was at already at Jeremy and Angela's bar-b-cueing. I finally stopped, changed shirts and went to the shower. John's mother walked in five minutes after me.

It was very awkward. John and I had nothing to do with one another in a room full of married couples, who we went to church with, and many of who had come to our house for our monthly couple get-togethers.

John eventually sneaked out after Angela yelled, "WHOEVER KEEP BUSTING THE BALLOONS, STOP!!!"

After I realized he was gone, I leaned over to Ms. Brenda, "Mom, where is John?"

"I don't know," she answered, as she looked around.

To avoid further embarrassment, I quietly hugged Angela and told her I was leaving to finish the house.

I waved to everyone when Angela's dad yelled, "Where is John?"

Embarrassed and tired, I responded, "I don't know," then I left.

About five minutes later, a furious Ms. Brenda called, "WHY DID YOU DO THAT? YOU DON'T EVER PUT PEOPLE IN YOUR BUSINESS. YOU ARE SUPPOSED TO COVER FOR YOUR HUSBAND! YOU DON'T EVER DO THAT…"

As I was driving back, **ALONE**, to the rent house that I only had ONE MORE DAY to finish before the new tenants were to move into, I stopped Ms. Brenda.

"Just a moment Ms. Brenda, but do you know where John is? Do you know where he was last night while I was at the rent house, with HIS DAUGHTER, until 1:00 in the morning while he was hanging out with Jeremy and Van bar-b-queing for a baby shower? Do you know he has only been out here to help me three times this whole week complaining, 'I told you not to get this house anyway?' Do you know, all week, I have worked at the salon in the day and at the rent house at night, while lying to everyone about John's whereabouts? I'M SICK OF COVERING FOR HIM so when you find him, you check HIM with this!"

CHAPTER 20

Anger, Against The Wrong Man

The fighting continued. Since I had a suite, I had a DVD/TV combo for movies, a small refrigerator with food, and since she often imitated me, I had a small area for Taylor to comb her baby dolls' hair. Taylor and I had come home from the shop a little after 7:30 p.m. to John sitting on the couch watching TV. I was exhausted and asked John if he would make Taylor a hotdog and run her bath water.

To my shock, JOHN WENT OFF, "I'M TIRED; YOU DO IT. IF YOU CAN'T HANDLE HER, YOU SHOULDN'T HAVE VOLUNTEERED TO KEEP HER FOR THE WHOLE MONTH."

"JOHN, ARE YOU SERIOUS? I'M ASKING YOU TO HELP ME WITH **YOUR** DAUGHTER AND YOU ARE MAD AT ME? I THOUGHT WE DISCUSSED THIS BECAUSE YOU WERE FINALLY ABLE TO SPEND TIME WITH HER, AND NOW YOU ARE MAD AT ME?" I protested in shock.

John answered, "WELL, JUST FORGET IT, I CAN TAKE TAYLOR OVER MY MOTHER'S HOUSE SINCE YOU ARE COMPLAINING!"

The next morning, I asked John if he would at least fix Taylor some cereal while I finished getting dressed for work.

John went off again, "YOU ARE THE ONE THAT ASKED HER MOM TO KEEP HER. I'M TRYING TO GET READY FOR AN INTERVIEW." (He was probably lying)

"JOHN, ARE YOU SERIOUS? OVER CEREAL??? I SEE WHY YOUR FAMILY CALL YOU LAZY! FORGET IT! I WILL GRAB SOMETHING WHILE WE'RE OUT!" I stated.

I was very angry while driving to work. The two lanes merged into one lane and a guy on a motorcycle attempted to cut me off. I had my blinker on but ignoring it, he sped up. Without stopping, I merged into the lane knocking the man off of his motorcycle. Then I pulled over, jumped out of the car and **snapped**, yelling, "WHAT THE H*LL IS WRONG WITH YOU? DIDN'T YOU SEE MY BLINKER? DIDN'T YOU SEE ME MERGING? WHAT IS WRONG WITH YOU???"

I never thought to check and see if the shocked, now limping man was okay.

I heard my three-year-old Taylor crying and screaming from her car seat, "TAKE ME TO MY NANA'S, TAKE ME TO MY NANA'S!"

I had never seen her that way, nor had she ever seen me behave the way I was behaving.

Hearing Taylor snapped me back. I recognized what I was doing and what I had just done to this innocent man. Why he was being silly or rude, had nothing to do with me. The rage against my husband, had nothing to do with him.

I realized I was going crazy. **I hit a man, then, I jumped out** of my car and **yelled at him** for it. I was out of character. I grew up seeing a lot of arguing and fighting, which is what shaped what used to be, my mild temperament. In the last four months, John had trained me to be a seasoned arguer with the bonus of now knowing how to cuss.

After calming down for a scared Taylor, I apologized to the man; the police let us both go. I drove to work trying to figure out who I had become. My mom's words had come to fruition.

CHAPTER 21

Airing Dirty Laundry

John and I had our fair share of arguing and making up, moving out and moving back in, but by this time, we had settled down. We were passionate about two things -- arguing and sex. It was so bad that I began to look for help. I wanted my marriage to work, so I began to search. The first counselor was a Christian professional whom I paid $95 an hour and we saw him twice.

"John, you will have to place boundaries on your relationship with your child's mother and the control she has." John thought he was biased.

The second counselor, I had to beg for because we were members of this church but because John was served there, he really was closed to being open. The third counselor was with the pastor of the church I attended with Mrs. Beverly prior to marrying John. John's mom felt we needed to be back at the church where John was serving. The next counselors were a pair, my client and her husband, who was a pastor. They counseled us, but then a day later, she talked about her husband being a mama's boy. After that, I could not figure if she was for or against mama's boys and mothers since she was a mother of all boys herself.

John and I were arguing to the point it seemed to be a three-ring circus. Cameron no longer felt comfortable around John and hated the way he treated and talked to me.

He never told me, but one day mom and I were talking, then she told me, "Cameron told Charles, 'John called our sister a B*tch.'"

Cameron was unhappy and began to rebel. He finally asked if he could move back to Oklahoma. I said okay. Although hurt, I understood.

"God is going to get you, man"

By this time, I was four months pregnant when John and I decided to see another marriage counselor, making this counselor number five. This one was very good friend of John's who was also a Pastor of a church. Our first meeting was with the pastor and the first lady at their home; it was more of getting to know the pastor and his family, socializing and them sharing their testimony. It was a good visit.

By the third visit, we surely had some things to discuss and I was ready. John and I had an argument the night before and I had discovered, on top of everything else we were there for, John's uncertainty of whether or not the baby I was carrying was his. Pastor Kirk and first lady sat there in silence for a second, staring at him. Then finally, pastor asked, "Why?"

He began, "Because we were into an argument one day and she told me to leave, so I did. But I came home somewhere close to midnight and she was gone..."

I cut in, "Pastor, first off, John failed to mention that we were arguing about Taylor's mom **again**. It was the weekend that my two cousins were in town to rehearse for my sister's play. They were **supposed** to stay at our house but not wanting my family to know that my husband wasn't coming home, I made it into a 'married girl's sleepover' with one of our high school classmates. I had asked if we could stay at her house making up a lie that Taylor was there sick. John, **he knew** that my family was coming in town and everyone was supposed to stay at our house, but he chose to pick a fight with me that weekend."

"Well, all I know is when I came home my wife, her pillow and her duffle bag were gone," John added.

"Pastor, so now John is saying this baby is not his?" I said holding my head down. My heart was broken. I had waited all this time to get married and have children with my husband, just for him to say that the baby I was carrying was not his.

Pastor Kirk looked to John for an explanation.

"I went through her dirty laundry and her panties were messy," John said.

Holding my head down in humiliation, with tears quietly falling from my face, I said, "Pastor, it was just vaginal discharge."

(It is actually known as leukorrhea which is common during pregnancy because of the increased presence of estrogen).

Pastor Kirk rose up from relaxing in his chair and in shock he asked, "WHAT?"

The first lady cut in and began to explain what happens to a woman's hormones when she becomes pregnant; although Pastor was in his 40s, their last child was a one-year-old.

Pastor Kirk knew about John allowing me to go to jail, about the Baby Mama Drama and the financial hardships from quitting and being fired from multiple jobs.

I guess this one did it for him because he finally found words, "John, God is going to get you, man, for the way you treat your wife."

BRINGING OTHERS INTO OUR MARRIAGE

Early in our marriage, John and I had made the terrible mistake of talking about past relationships. My mother WARNED me against this many years prior to meeting John.

I would feel less than a woman because I was **not** producing much natural lubrication. John and I were in a conversation about past relationships and I told him how I used to naturally produce so much, that it was called "ooze." John recalled one relationship where there was a woman that "would get so wet." After that moment, I compared myself to a woman that I didn't even know.

I was twenty-nine years old when this sequence of events took place: November 21, I bought my first home, December 21, I gained custody of my eleven-year-old paternal baby brother, and January 21, I met John.

Somewhere after, something had happened to my body; the "ooze" was no more and I was ashamed. but John and I would buy lubrication. So, when I became pregnant, I produced everything times two. I felt like a normal again. You would have thought John would've been happy; instead, he chose to humiliate me.

CHAPTER 22

FIRED AGAIN: Pole

Mom was over visiting. We were chatting about an outing John and I had gone on with some friends when she cut in and asked how John was doing on his new valet job. I told her that he had quit that one because he'd began making more money at the first job. She made no comment. I continued to talk about the outing until she couldn't take it anymore.

She informed me, "Tori, can I tell you something? John didn't quit; he was fired. Remember when he had told you about him hitting a pole with a car? Well, it was one of the doctor's Mercedes."

My sister had confided in my mom that she felt bad because her friend hired John as a favor to her because I was pregnant and I needed help and insurance. Now, her sorority sister, colleague and friend was being questioned by her manager for hiring him.

I knew about the incident but I did not know he was FIRED for it; he continued to leave every day for his first and second job. Plus, we had discussed him quitting that job because he had finally begun making more money at the first job. He was insistent on quitting, but I was concerned about the insurance benefits because I was pregnant but John encouraged me, "Go ahead and get yourself on Medicaid, WIC and food stamps. That's what

THE DIVORCE

everyone else does when they get pregnant. That's what Deirdre did and Medicaid paid for everything."

By this time, as a hairstylist, I had no insurance and John was an independent contractor/idle laborer, so I had no choice but to apply for government assistance.

Wow, Wow, WOW! Fired again? And to make it worse, I HAD TO HEAR IT **FROM MY MOM WHO KNEW** my husband had just **LIED TO ME.** Getting fired again **AND** lying to **me?** *WHAT WAS HE THINKING?* Lying to me in the presence of our enemies, I had no words. There was no way I could cover for him. These two acts were public and he did not prepare me for it by telling me the truth.

John had come home by now and mom asked him about his new job and they chatted for a second. After she left, I asked:

"John, did you get fired from the Hospital?" I questioned.

"Naw, who told you that?" he responded.

"John, did you get fired for hitting a doctor's Mercedes?" I asked.

"No, Tori, remember, I told you I quit," he answered, "Remember, I told you that they must've put a pole behind it so I hit it."

I saw those dark clouds hover the earth.

I asked, "So, you're telling me that when you parked the car there was no pole? After that, someone sent for concrete mix, poured it behind the car **you** parked, placed a pole there, stabilized it and dried it?"

I didn't know if I had it in me to be embarrassed anymore. In fact, embarrassment had moved on.

I got to the point where, I just didn't care. I was married to him. He was my husband. I went in knowing that he needed help and I was going to stick by him.

CHAPTER 23

FIRED AGAIN: Chicken and Dumplings

Since John had been fired from this part-time job, he was now able to work full-time.

One day, John came in LIVID.

"TORI, SOME WOMAN CALLED THE POLICE ON ME," he yelled as he paced the floor.

"John, what happened?" I calmly asked, thinking it was the usual; he either took someone's equipment or he had broken something. I laid across the bed to hear this story, but I WAS NOT prepared for what was coming next.

He sat down and began, "See, I was working on this lady's roof and I had to use the restroom. So, I went in and asked if I could use it. She said, yeah. When I came out, I noticed she was cooking chicken and dumplings and I just told her it smelled good. She invited me to eat with her, so I did."

I sat up as I began to see the dark cloud hover the earth and my blood began to boil.

He continued, "So, while we were eating, she started talking to me about her ex-husband, and her divorce, and the kids and all kinds of stuff. So, I just started talking encouraging her. When I was getting ready to leave, I leaned over and kissed her on the forehead. I left and went to my next location. Next thing I know, the police pulled up behind my truck asking questions and talking about this lady accusing me of trying to kiss her."

I could neither move nor talk. I was in complete and utter SHOCK. I finally got enough air in my lungs and stomach to ask, "You had lunch with her?"

"Well, see," he tried to answer, but I cut him off.

"WAIT! Did you have lunch with HER?" I demanded, determined to get a straight answer.

"Naw, she just offered me something to eat and I was going to take it outside, but she wanted me to eat at the table," he replied.

"So, the answer is 'YES!' You did have lunch with her?" I asked hoping he would own up.

He tried to convince me, "Well, not really because..."

"JOHN, STOP!" I yelled with my eyes closed and one hand up; I couldn't stand the very sight of him. "You know how your mom and siblings call you 'stupid' when you do things that make absolutely no sense? Well, you say you didn't kiss her, so that means you've gotten fired over CHICKEN AND DUMPLINGS???"

CHAPTER 24

The Thought Was Nice But...

It was a Saturday afternoon and I was seven months pregnant; tired, stressed and very busy, so I called mom to come and shampoo my clients' hair. John had been calling and checking on me, but finally, I had to let him know that I was very busy and I couldn't continue to stop and answer the phone.

John did the strangest thing; he began to yell at me, "I WAS JUST CALLING TO CHECK ON YOU AND SEE HOW YOUR DAY WAS GOING," then he hung up.

Baffled, I remained calm and continued to work.

Minutes later, a man from Edible Arrangements stepped in, "Hi, I have a delivery for Tori Knight?"

I stood there in shock.

Mom said, "Tori, that's you!"

I stood there.

He looked on the card attached and said, "It's from your husband?"

I finally thanked the man and received the DELICIOUS CELEBRATION® SWIZZLE SAMPLER. This dish was filled and decorated with cantaloupe and honeydew wedges, Kale, grapes, pineapple stars and daisies, chocolate dipped strawberries and apples all beautifully arranged. The clients "oohed and awed" and sighed while the only thing I could think of was *this chicken and dumpling eating dipstick has **just been fired**; and now that he* *received his last paycheck, HE SPENDS IT ON THIS. WE HAVE BILLS, CHILD SUPPORT, CAR NOTES AND A BABY ON THE WAY, WHICH MEANS I AM GOING TO HAVE TO STOP WORKING FOR A MOMENT. AND CURRENTLY, HE HAS NO JOB. WHAT WAS HE THINKING???*

Of course, I didn't react. My mom was aware that I was carrying the load because John refused to keep a job. I knew she was thinking all the things that I was thinking, but I was not about to entertain her. I smiled on the outside while feeling sick on the inside wondering, *how much did this dish cost* **ME**?

I figured out John's reason for snapping. It's because he was expecting a reaction from the delivery, but I had not received it yet. Not wanting a scene, I kindly sent him a "Thank you, baby. I love it," text.

I continued to pretend I was excited until the next day, when he called about buying me a $75 Coach diaper bag.

"I don't need that sweetie but thank you," I declared.

"WHY?" he asked offensively.

"Well, first of all, because we need the money right now. Second, it's fake," I answered.

"No, it's not! And if it is, it's no different than all those other fake purses you be wearing!" he retaliated.

"John, all my purses are real, including the one I gave your mother," I countered.

"Well, your grandmother shops at thrift stores!" he revenged.

That was below the belt. At that time, my grandmother, who is my heart, was deathly ill and John knew it.

THE DIVORCE

Because I was at the kitchen table eating with mom, I hung up the phone and I answered via text, "Look, you brought nothing and you came from nothing. Don't you ever talk about my grandmother again!"

A few weeks later, I noticed that I had received NO calls from his mom. Needless to say, John showed her that text message. That was the straw that broke the camel's back; Ms. Brenda and I were finished.

CHAPTER 25

OUR HOUSE GUESTS: My Mom and My Youngest Brother

In the midst of all that John and I were going through, my mom was in the midst of losing everything. She was devastated because everything she had known for the past four years was suddenly gone in thirty days. In just thirty days, my mom had lost her home, her clothes ministry, her car and her job. She had lost the home that she had been renting for more than four years because suddenly the landlord decided to sell it. Her car was repossessed because she had been financially helping out a family member, who had promised to repay her once they received their income tax refund. On top of all of that, she had suddenly been laid off of the job she had been working on for two years without notice. But worst of all, in that house that she had rented, was where my mother's clothes closet ministry was housed. This is where people were able to come and get the help they needed. There was an abundance of donations from friends, families, churches and church members. She and my fourteen-year-old brother moved in with my sister. Needless to say, it didn't work out. She didn't have the space. I, who had the space, asked her to move in with us. I knew it was a bad idea because of how she felt about John, but I couldn't stand the thought of her and my brother bouncing around because of her pride. Finally, she agreed.

However, that did not come without a price. DAILY, my mom nagged, "John should be doing this. A husband is supposed to do that. Your yard has trash in it. Where is John? You shouldn't be stressed out about this..."

Not only did she complain about what John was or wasn't doing, she and my brother weren't doing them either. One morning, mom told me some trash had blown into the yard and the yard needed to be raked. That evening, my mom came in and found me lying in bed. She complimented the yard but was confused on how it had gotten that way.

I admitted, "Mom, I did it."

Seemingly in shock she said, "TORI, YOU ARE EIGHT MONTHS PREGNANT!"

I answered, "Yes, but you said it needed to be done. John was at work and you told me that Charles is not my husband, so don't ask him to do anything for me; so I did it."

CHAPTER 26

FIRED AGAIN: GAS

Around the time when I was about six and a half months pregnant, John left the house every day claiming to go to work. The problem was by this time, many weeks had passed and John still had not brought home a paycheck. I called my weekly client Rachel, who was a recruiter, and asked her if she could get him a job. She empathized with me because by this time, I was pregnant and was carrying the entire load. We used to talk about our similar situations where we both were the providers and our "Mama's boy" husbands were having problems staying employed. She finally left her husband, one year after having their baby boy.

I called John to come home and talked to him about his "working for free" jobs; I encouraged him to call Rachel. He called and talked to her about his work experience and emailed his resume to her. She set up an interview for the following day; John aced it. **She did me the favor** of not only finding him a job, but she found him a supervisor's position. The job was an hour away, but it paid well.

Not Again, John!

Everything seemed to be going well. John was bringing in a steady paycheck and contributed to the house financially, which took a lot of pressure off of me being pregnant. Going into my eighth month of pregnancy, I began to slow down on working and being on my feet. I wanted to be home with my brand new baby for the first four weeks of her life. Then, work part-time afterward, so she would not be in day care for the first year of her life. John and I discussed and agreed on this plan.

About three months later, Rachel called, "Tori, I'm sorry to bother you because I know you're pregnant, but has John called you?"

"Yes, he did about someone trying to frame him," I responded. But **knowing** my husband, I asked, "Rachel, what happened?"

"Well, John is on his way to turn in his badges..." she started as the story began to unfold. John had been on that job about four weeks when apparently, Rachel started receiving phone calls from the client that her company had sent John to work for. Not only did they realize that John didn't know what the heck he was doing, but he was making some of the female employees "uncomfortable." Of course, Rachel never told me anything was going on. I remained quiet as she continued because now his desire to stay late for "overtime" began to make sense. Then, she mentioned theft.

"THEFT???" I shouted in shock.

She urged me to calm down while reminding me that I was pregnant and that *my* husband was the same husband that allowed me to go to jail.

I thanked Rachel for the heads up and I apologized profusely for my husband's actions. My friend and client did me a favor and this was our repayment.

And 5,4,3,2...

"THEY'RE TALKING ABOUT LETTING ME GO FOR BORROWING GAS!" John yelled as he walked in the door irate.

I calmly questioned, "Borrowing gas? How did you get someone to loan you GAS?"

"Because they said I was putting gas in my truck using the company's credit card," he answered. "That's an hour drive back-and-forth. I kept the receipt, so that I could pay them back on my next pay check. Shoot, my mom said that if I didn't have any intentions on paying them back that would have been stealing and they should've given me the opportunity to pay them back. At least, I wasn't calling in like some people do; I was just trying to get back-and-forth to work."

In my head, I heard thunder as the dark cloud hover the earth, I asked, "SO THAT'S WHERE YOU HAVE BEEN? CRYING TO YOUR MOMMY?"

Not giving him a chance to answer, I asked, "Where is the receipt? I will have to pay it because Rachel is my client and my friend who did ME a favor, the client that comes every week, sometimes twice, she just *gave* us her baby equipment because you know we don't have any extra money to go buy any. YOU JUST PUT HER JOB ON THE LINE. How much is it for in the first place?"

He answered, "They say it was for $207."

In shock, I yelled, "$207??? HOW THE H*LL, DO YOU PUT $207 IN A 2000 MOUNTAINEER? ARE YOU SERIOUS? THAT'S

NOT STEALING, THAT'S GRAND THEFT AUTO! HOW MANY CARS WERE YOU FUELING UP?"

I calmed down and once again said, "John, you know how your mom and sisters call you 'stupid' when you do things that make absolutely no sense? You say you weren't stealing, so that means you've gotten fired for 'BORROWING GAS!'"

CHAPTER 27

FIRED + ARRESTED = LABOR

One week after John was fired, he ran a stop sign and was pulled over and arrested in front of our home for warrants after the cops ran his driver's license. He used all the money in our joint account, bailed himself out and headed back; he had only been gone two hours. But before he made it home, my mom began telling me, with urgency, to remove or hide his guns because she felt he was going to come back and harm everyone in the house. She asked me to go with her, but I refused, so she and my brother left.

Seconds after driving off, she called, "John is outside hiding behind your bushes."

Now, I know that he heard my mom urging me to leave with them because she felt he was going to kill everybody. How long had he been out there? And why?

I did not sleep that night. Not one wink. What's worse -- labor pain or a toothache? I was in so much pain. My back had a dull pain. Any position I lay in was worse than the first. My stomach was cramping like crazy. It felt like I was extremely constipated, but having menstrual cramps at the same time. My hip felt like I was lying directly on the bone. The bed felt like cement. John asked a few times was I okay, and I would say, yes, because I didn't want to disturb him, but I couldn't believe the pain my back, my stomach, MY BODY was in. Every inch of me! I would have rather passed out.

Around 7:00 that morning, my mother called (I guess to see if I was still alive). I told her and my sister that I hadn't slept because my back was in pain.

My sister in the background said, "She may be having back labor."

It just so happened that I had a doctor's appointment and mom met John and I there. I had just turned thirty-six weeks pregnant that day.

I told the nurse what was going on, the doctor checked me and said, "You are 3-4 centimeters dilated, head over to the hospital."

Scene I: And 5, 4, 3, 2…

"DOCTOR, ARE WE ABOUT TO HAVE A BABY??? MY WIFE IS IN LABOR??? OH, LORD! OH, MY GOD! MY WIFE IS IN LABOR! WE GONNA HAVE A BABY!!!"

Someone had gotten my mom, who walked in, seeing me sitting on the table, "You're getting ready to have the baby?" she asked. But before I answered, my eyes led hers to John, who was surrounded by four nurses: two on each side of him, one on his right side, talking very slowly trying to calm him down, another on that same side, but kneeling down fanning him. On his left side, was a nurse kneeling down trying to get him to drink orange juice and the other was standing beside him with a paper bag for him to calm down and breathe. Mom looked back at me and rolled her eyes:

"Get John's mom on the phone," Mom said disgustedly. "Brenda, hi, this is Jerri, I wanted to let you know that Tori's in labor...yes, she's fine, she's just sitting here, but John may need you... Well..." and she went on to describe what she was witnessing. Suddenly, mom burst into a silent laughter (the kind you have in church), not to disturb the nurses and John, then she passed the phone to me.

I said, "Hello?"

Brenda yelled, "TELL JOHN TO GET HIS HIPS SOMEWHERE AND SIT DOWN; THIS AIN'T ABOUT HIM!!!"

Scene II: And 5,4,3,2...

Twelve hours later, a healthy, six pound baby girl was born. Immediately, John BURSTS into tears of joy -- LOUDLY. Literally, John was leaned over on my pillow, boo-hooing in my ear, while he rubbed my hair. The nurses were "oohing and awing," my sister was snapping pictures; my mom was excited-turned-disgusted as the nurses congratulated the emotional "new" father. I laid there wondering, *did John forget that we're married and that I am very aware that he HAS a daughter and was present for her birth?* If I didn't know him, you would have thought this was his first experience because of the way he was carrying on.

She came at thirty-six weeks, and besides Jaundice, she was PERFECT. My mom and sister kept trying to get me to hold her, but they couldn't understand that I was afraid. I had NO sleep the night before and I had just endured twelve hours of labor and ten of those twelve were without medication.

I was on a lot of meds and was very, very tired from no sleep from the night before, plus twelve hours of labor. On top of that, the nurses woke me up every two hours to feed the baby. John would get up with me every two hours to coach me and to listen to what the nurses was saying, so he'd be able to help me when we got home or feed the baby himself. He was such the proud father. He was proud of being experienced, too, because he was able to let the nurses see that he already knew some things. It was funny to watch him being so proud, passing out pink bubble gum cigars to the staff, feeding, changing, walking, singing, bouncing and cuddling our daughter. I didn't have to lift a finger. Not only was he spoiling her, he was spoiling me, too. Although many times, I had to beg for him to give me turns to hold the baby.

We talked and laughed. As he sat there with a pink bubble gum cigar hanging out the side of his mouth, people called to congratulate us and he called random people to tell them, "Me and my wife just had a baby!"

At one point, he, holding Jaden, came and kissed me on my forehead and said, "Baby, this is the way it's **supposed** to be; this is the way God meant for it to be."

The day after our daughter was born, the hospital staff brought a round table, chairs, white table cloth and cloth napkins; then came glasses, deserts, salads and dinnerware covered with silver tops. They put the baby down and helped me off the bed to the chair. The lady, who delivered the food, pulled the tops off the dishes for John and me and there were two dishes: one with steak, mashed potatoes, gravy, asparagus and dinner rolls. The other plate had lobster, mashed potatoes, gravy and asparagus. John was cheesing and his eyes were big. My eyes began to well as John and I held hands under the table and our daughter slept peacefully beside the table.

When the lady walked out, John looked me in the eyes and said, "Baby, this is the way it's supposed to be; me, my wife and my baby."

Later, I asked, didn't the hospital where Taylor was born do this with you and Deirdre when you two had her? He said, no, because they weren't married.

Again, every two hours, I was told to nurse Jaden for my breast milk to come down. Sadly, it was still clear. The nurses continued to encourage me, "Don't worry, it'll come. Sometimes it takes a few days. Just stay with it."

In the meantime, they also supplemented with the courtesy of two ounce milks that labor and delivery provided. Little Jaden would be pleased, but I was concerned because I had read books that cautioned away from nipple confusion. There are nipples that allow the milk to come out fast and freely, whereas when a baby sucks from the breast, they have to work for it.

I was a mother and a mother gives her child the very best. Breast milk was the very best milk, so I was determined to give her that. The problem was I was not producing enough milk. I was crushed. The nurses gave me hope that if I pumped and breast fed often, my milk would come in. We had an appointment scheduled with the lactation nurse, who I met with, the day after I left the hospital. I was excited because now it had been three days and all my baby was getting was this clear liquid from my breast. I HAD tried everything. I had watched the videos that WIC had gave me, I had read the Expecting book, I had pumped and breastfed every hour, I drank Mother's Milk tea, took the prescription medications, and finally, I tried beer (nurse recommended). Eventually, I was able to pump out 2-6 ounces per **day**.

My heart was broken when John and mom, shockingly came together, and told me the reasons why my baby was so fussy. She was hungry and we **had to** supplement. I was devastated, hurt and confused. I was concerned about bonding with my baby through breast feeding, nipple confusion, and if she would she reject me if my full supply of milk finally came in. I cried upstairs while understanding the crying had stopped because she was finally eating. I knew she needed it, especially with her having Jaundice.

CHAPTER 28

The Crumble

I went back to work **THIRTEEN DAYS** AFTER DELIVERY. The bills were due and once again, John couldn't contribute, so yes, THIRTEEN DAYS after I delivered my first child, I was back on my feet working. I had already left the salon suite, where I had been working, just a week before giving birth because I wanted to stay home with my new baby for a minimum of six months to a year. John and I had discussed and agreed on that; he would be the provider during this time. My siblings and I had never been to daycare as infants, so I could not see my children going as infants either. I didn't want to cut hair, deal with chemicals and styling agents in my home because for one, I had a newborn and two, it was my home. But unfortunately, I had to provide so I could pay our utilities on time. We had NO extra money because John had bailed himself out of jail the night before Jaden was born. I called only a select few clients to see if they would let me do their hair at my house so I could rest **and** pay the bills. Fortunately, they agreed.

19 DAYS After Giving Birth

NINETEEN DAYS after giving birth, John asked me for sex; I declined. Physically, I had JUST HAD A BABY and was already working. Mentally, I was exhausted because I was carrying the entire load. He became angry, so later on, he left "to go find a job."

THE DIVORCE

A few hours later, I noticed something telling. In our nightstand drawer, out of our baby shower gag gift which was a package of three condoms, one condom was missing. I began to lose it. So now, on top of today's stress of mom complaining about John, I had to suffer in silence and wonder, *where is this condom*?

John finally came home and of course, mom, who felt John was going to kill us all, wanted to leave. I was determined to stay. After her begging, I allowed her to take my baby, and then she and my brother left.

He went upstairs and cut the TV on. I began questioning him about the condom. He ignored me. Now infuriated, I declared, "You can either tell me where that condom is or you get out!"

John began to yell, "I'M NOT GOING ANYWHERE! I'M NOT GOING ANYWHERE!!"

I went downstairs and called my Apostle Roberts so that neither John nor I would do anything that would cause me to go to jail and leave my new baby girl. Upon answering, all Apostle Roberts could hear was John SCREAMING and CURSING at me. Apostle Roberts continued to keep me calm hoping that at any moment, John would stop before the ranting and raving became physical again. John finally stopped long enough to hear me telling the Pastor that this all started because I asked him about a missing condom. Wow! It was brand new. John started going off ALL OVER AGAIN. He finally came downstairs and brought me a torn condom wrapper:

I asked, "John, why was the condom missing?"

He angrily responded, "I USED IT ON MYSELF!!!"

"On yourself??" I questioned.

"YEAH, SINCE YOU WOULDN'T GIVE ME NONE, I WENT DOWNSTAIRS AND USED IT ON MYSELF SO I WOULDN'T MAKE A MESS!!!" he shouted.

I asked, "So, where is the condom?"

He shouted, "IT'S IN THE TOILET, STUPID!!!"

I calmly said, "Do you hear him Apostle?"

John did a double take and walked away apparently embarrassed.

Apostle continued to advise me, "Don't say anything back because you don't want to go back to jail and you know that he **will** allow the police to take you. Do not say anything back. I'm here; I'm praying."

A few minutes later, John came downstairs with a duffle bag and left.

I called my mom shortly after with news that would make her evening, "Mom, you guys can come back. John left."

I hung up and fell to the floor and cried. I laid on the kitchen floor in a fetal position holding my stomach because this cry was coming from the pit of my gut. I could only hope the neighbors could not hear my wailing, but I felt like I was going to die. I knew my mom was less than ten minutes away so finally I got up, and washed my face and combed my hair.

Mom, Jaden and Charles was back and approximately two minutes later, there was a knock at the door. Mom warned me that John came back to kill us.

I called his cell and asked, "What do you want?"

He answered, "I need gas money."

I gave John $10 and shut the door.

Two days later, my account had two $35 overdrafts. John had not only taken the $10 I had given him, but with the money in our account he also filled his truck up at the gas station without my knowledge. So, I was unable to cover the account for other purchases due to come out of the account that day.

CHAPTER 29

POSTPARTUM DEPRESSION

I made an appointment with my doctor. I realized my maternal instincts had not kicked in, or had left. I knew something was wrong. I leaned over and kissed my baby Jaden, who was asleep in the cradle swing, and I walked out of the door. My mom, sensing something was wrong, tried to call my cell; I turned it off. I cried all the way to my appointment.

With my breast milk not coming in, the separation from my husband, having gone back to work so soon, not being able to bond with my baby, the strained relationship with my mom, and the stress over bills, I was propelled into full-blown postpartum depression. One minute, I was a married new mother; the next, I was performing as a single mother of a nineteen day old newborn.

With all of this, I felt like a failure. The enemy began to have fun with my mind saying, "Your baby doesn't know you and she only wants her grandma, your husband doesn't want you, where's the condom, what type of mother goes back to work after having a baby, look at the way your mother looks at you, you are such a disappointment. You can't even produce enough milk to feed her. Go drop her off at the fire station so that you won't burden your mother with the responsibility that you couldn't handle. You can end this misery by taking pills. It's painless. You will finally get the sleep you desire; calm peaceful sleep. You will never wake up to this misery. You will sleep in eternal peace." This sounded so comforting and soothing. I began to relax knowing my way out.

Obviously my mother called Apostle Roberts knowing my love and respect for him as my pastor and "father." She was troubled by the words I said to my daughter before I left, "I will always love you." While in the waiting room of the doctor's office Apostle Roberts, a seasoned wise pastor, called and cut right to the chase, "Hey daughter, your mom just called me, can you talk?" I answered yes, but he tricked me and went right into praying. Sometimes, people will ask can they pray with you. He didn't. Had he asked first, I would've said no. When he gets mad at the devil, there are no questions or negotiations. The gloves are off.

CHAPTER 30

THE FAMILIES:

His side

A few days after the separation, I called Brenda and asked her how John was doing.

She angrily began to tell me how at peace he was and how she told him, "Everybody I know has been divorced at least once!"

I was shocked.

"You told him that???" I asked.

I could definitely hear the anger in her voice as she continued, "I told him to stay here and get his money together, then in two months get an apartment."

Where did she and I go wrong??? John warned me early on in the relationship to, "STOP TALKING TO MY MOM." Deirdre also warned me, "Be careful, she and I were close once before too, but... that's her baby."

She and I were very tight: We'd sat together in church, go shopping together, and have fun with Taylor. She cooked every Sunday. She would spend the night and we would sit up talking for hours.

John's sister and I had a decent relationship also, but by this time, it was our third separation and maybe the fifth time I had his cell phone disconnected. Needless to say our relationship had soured. In fact, this is an excerpt of the email I received from her:

"Life is all about making choices. Sometimes we make the right ones and other times we don't... A few years ago you made a choice that you should have put a little more thought into. I don't, by any stretch of the imagination, think that my brother is or was perfect. But, you knew that when you chose to marry him. Nevertheless, you wanted to be married so desperately that you were willing to accept ANYTHING... ...Well, hopefully this time he will be smart enough to stay away. You've manipulated him long enough. Every time you decide you are tired of putting up with him you chose to kick him out... You remember, he is nothing and he came from nothing...While he is not perfect, it seems that you are full of bad decisions. You are just as much to blame as he is...We don't hate your baby... So now that he is gone, that means his family is gone as well...You've made your bed, now sleep in it. This is the life you chose, now deal with it. We don't hate your baby. John tries to come and see your baby, so he represents our entire family. Besides, we have our hands full trying to reverse the effects on Taylor that your actions have caused. We certainly wouldn't want that baby to take time."

After I read that email to my mom, I read her my reply.

Which read in part, "I'm very sorry for the hurt. I purposely waited to reply to give you time and hopefully catch you in good spirits... [John] adores you. In the entire two years we'd been together, [he] HAS NEVER, EVER said ANYTHING negative about you nor to you. Not even the times you've publicly made a fool of him when he's pronounced words wrong. I have ALWAYS chosen to see the good in people. Many times that has gotten me into trouble but I married John because of his heart. He told me his dreams and aspirations, and like many testimonies...I believed that I could help him reach them...I didn't realize that HIS OWN FAMILY had no faith in him either. I do remember vividly, the very first time you and I met...you said, 'don't get pregnant by him.' YES, You did warn me...In your letter, you said I was, '<u>desperate</u> for marrying your brother who you called <u>anything</u>...' and continued, 'you should have waited to learn what we already knew' ...Now for the SAD part...DEGRADATION is so normal for him that he called that letter having his back... [He] loves you unconditionally and always chose to see the good in you. That's why it saddened me to read such disparagement from YOU....If he hears the words, 'you stupid, you sorry, big punk...' then he's going to behave in that manner... and he will always draw out the negative in people (employers, girlfriends, wives, friends, family, LIFE) because that's a norm for him.. ...John has great potential. As his sister that's with him often, begin to reverse that. Start speaking positives & words of encouragement. Encourage him to build a stronger foundation in Christ so he can see himself as Christ sees him & he won't pass that spirit to his children... You never have to see me again but John is your brother for the rest of your life. Please ask GOD to show you how to love and see him the way he loves and sees you. - 1 Cor 13:4-8"

(Sadly, her response to my reply was worse than the first email she had sent. Shocked, I did not reply. Unfortunately for John, I used the emails against him in court.)

My side

Mom proudly said, "Wow, Tori, that was very nice of you to have responded in love. Send that to me so that I can show my friends."

I emailed her the correspondence.

A few days and upsets later, she informed me, "His sister told the truth. She said what everybody else has been thinking all along but didn't want to say to you. Even Ken, (my older brother) said, 'Mom, she wasn't lying, that is John and he has not changed.'"

Sadly, I discovered that the email was to confirm to everyone what mom had been telling them. Basically, I was stupid and don't make good decisions. Her wanting me to send that email to her had nothing to do with the fact that I "responded in love." I was hurt and embarrassed that my mom's resentment for my marriage would let her go to this extent.

Despite the embarrassment and hurt feelings, and our relationship between each other, my mother was truly an angel to my daughter. She fed, clothed, bathed and sang to her. She kept her in the daytime so I could work, and kept her at night so I could sleep to be able to go to work the next day.

CHAPTER 31

BUT, HE WAS MY HUSBAND!

John and I had been separated two months. He had visited Jaden and me a few times and I always felt privileged because I missed him and wanted him back.

There was a day that John came to visit and as usual, when I heard his voice, my heart melted, *HE'S HERE*! My mom told John that I was upstairs; I could feel my heart pounding as I heard each step. He came up and found me lying in the bed with our daughter sleeping on my chest. We talked briefly, and then suddenly he wanted sex. Although he was my husband and I was excited to see him, I refused because he was not home with me, so there's a possibility that he was "out there." I could not allow him to treat me like a baby mama or side chick anymore. I was his wife and there were many days when I thought about the time he would come home, I could just lie on his chest and he would just hold me because he loved me. Or maybe we'd be in bed and he would hold our daughter while my head would lie on his shoulder. He would recognize that I was tired and had been on my feet working; then cooking, feeding, changing diapers, mixing formula, waking up all times of the night, picking up toys, or stretching myself so that the toddler wouldn't feel neglected as she required so much of my time. He would just simply rub my feet or take the girls for a walk so that I could have at least one hour to do whatever I wanted.

John began kissing me. "You come have sex with me then go home or where ever? No, this has got to stop. I can't ALLOW you to continue to have your cake and eat it, too," I told him.

He tried again. I refused. Then, I reminded him that I had the BABY ON MY CHEST (as if the blood that was leaving his head caused blindness and he couldn't see her). I loved him so it hurt me to reject him, but the feelings of rejection, being used and hurt after he would get up and leave, I didn't want to feel that anymore.

Then, MY phone rang. It was a new client. BINGO. John began to pry my left hand away from my shorts that was gripping them, as I talked on the phone with the other hand, but eventually he succeeded. With our sleeping baby on my chest, he began to perform oral sex on me while I was still on the phone taking the appointment. I ended the call quickly as I felt the "volcano about to erupt."

As soon as I dropped the phone (I can only *hope* that she had hung up) POW! I was torn by the fact that I loved and wanted my husband, but I couldn't bear to feel that emptiness I would feel as I'd watch him get up, get dressed and LEAVE.

"John, why did you do that?" I asked.

He didn't respond as he, already between my legs, began to climb upon me.

"John stop, STOP!" I told him.

He didn't say anything.

"Stop!" I quietly uttered to him as I tried not to wake my sleeping baby on my chest and aware that my mom, who couldn't stand him, was downstairs in my open-floor-plan den.

He tried to insert himself as I pushed my body back until my head was against the headboard. He inserted.

"John, stop. STOP! You can't keep doing this to me. John, get up now, stop," I said to him as I struggled to get him *out* of me, with a baby sleeping on my chest.

He *came* and got up and began putting his pants on. I laid there in silence. I couldn't move because I was in shock. I guess he realized I was serious; he looked at me, then sat on the edge of the bed with his head down. I recognized that since we had a very active sex life in our marriage, I had NEVER rejected him, and he knew how I felt about my wifely duties according to the Bible, that he didn't take me serious.

"John, I told you to stop. Why didn't you stop?" He sat there in silence and then:

"I'm so ashamed of myself," he said.

"What now? What should I think now?" I asked.

"Call the police?" he answered.

He sat there in silence for a few minutes. I laid there staring at him. He gave a heartfelt apology and left. There were a million thoughts going through my head, *He was my best friend, my husband, and my child's father. How could I have him put in jail? Then, he will never want to come back to us. I wouldn't want him to feel the feeling of betrayal and hurt that I felt when he allowed me to go to jail. Maybe I should have yelled, "No!" Well, if I had done that, mom would have an excuse to come in and stab him. Maybe I shouldn't have taken that call. I do need the money to take care of us, but I didn't have to answer that phone. Well, when it all boils down to it, he is my husband and I shouldn't have rejected my husband.* I cried as the thoughts swam in my head. Eventually I fell asleep.

CHAPTER 32

Together! AGAIN???

After being separated for almost three months, we began spending time with our mentors, Beverly and Allen, who had convinced us to get back together and to not focus on our problems, but trust GOD to be the Problem-solver.

As we began to meet and spend more time together, my mom gave me an ultimatum, "If you and John get back together, I'm leaving."

My neighbors were going on a camping trip and asked us to come along for they felt it'd be good for our troubled marriage. They paid for EVERYTHING and we had a blast.

Upon our return, we were due for our counseling session with the Pastor Tony and Co-pastor Mary, the pastors of the church I was a member of. Pastor Tony asked why we didn't go to counseling at the church where John had been serving for eleven years and where we had been members. I informed him that John didn't want to because he was serving there.

Pastor asked John, "When you lived with your daughter's mother, did you continue to go to church."

"Yes," John answered.

"Did you continue to serve?" Pastor asked.

"Yes," John proudly answered.

Pastor responded, "You should not have. You should have sat down at that time; you should have been getting fed. You were serving under a seasoned pastor while secretly knowing you were living with your pregnant girlfriend." John had no words.

I brought up the fact that a few days prior to our meeting, a lady called his cell at 11:40 p.m. and John refused to tell her that he was back home with his wife.

John expressed, "Well, I won't tell them we got back together just in case she put me out again."

The pastor seriously retorted, "You cannot be back with your wife and have a third wheel."

John began to justify and make excuses for his actions as smoke began to steam from my ears. Pastor Mary looked at me, noticing the change in my demeanor asked with a smirk, "Are you okay?"

I answered, "Yes, I just need to get John back to his car, so he can move back with his mom and continue with his women." And that I did.

AGAIN

One week after our counseling session with Pastors Tony and Mary, John called Beverly and Allen asking for help on getting his family back. They called me and I came. We had a very good conversation and he expressed his love and need for his family and his desire to be come back home. At the end, we left and went home -- together. One week after John and I reconciled, my mom moved out as promised.

Being back together, **again**, John and I had a lot of happy sex. It was a few times per day so on day three of our reconciliation, I called John on his cell, "John, stop by the store and get some condoms; I'm ovulating."

He responded in shock, "CONDOMS? I AIN'T USIN' NO CONDOMS ON MY WIFE!!!"

I warned, "Okay, if I get pregnant, I don't want to hear your mouth!"

A few weeks passed and sure enough, one morning, a little after midnight, John woke out of his sleep and then woke me up out of mine and asked, "Tori, did you get your period this month?"

Frustrated that he woke me up, I responded, "John, what are you talking about *my* period for? I don't ask you about your period! Go back to sleep!"

The next morning, I woke up and thought about it, ***did*** *I have my period???*

I took the test a few days and arguments later. I left the test in the bathroom for the three minutes indicated.

John went in, then, he comes out pimp walking, "I'm fixing to go buy some blue paint for my son's room!"

Of course, since we already had two girls, we were hoping for the boy that we had been prophesied about. A few days later, I asked him about his waking up through the night inquiring about my cycle and he told me, "God told me that you were pregnant and that it was a boy."

CHAPTER 33

UNUSUAL BEHAVIOR

A week later, John and I were having an argument. In the argument, John began to call me names, "stupid" and "dumb." I finally retorted, "Your family will think I'm stupid for getting pregnant by you again!" John hit me with the bus driver upper cut by saying, "YOU NEED TO HAVE AN ABORTION!"

I paused in shock. I had no comeback, just shock. No hurt, no pain; just a blank stare. Finally, I said, "You serve in church every Sunday and you suggest that your wife have an abortion?"

A month went by and we seemed, well, just okay. I did notice that every evening he was going to the "library" to check his emails. *Hmmm, he already has a job, why would he need to spend an hour at the library **every day** before coming home?* I thought. I was aware that his classmates and rival schools were having an alumni mixer, and unlike past years, he wanted to go this year, with "the fellas."

I asked him, "What fellas, John? Who? When did you start hanging out with the fellas?"

He had lame excuses, but I knew my husband. We did everything together. Everything! Not saying that people cannot have their own set of friends, but we started out doing everything together, by his choice. I enjoyed hanging out with my husband and best friend, but I was always willing to give him his space. Sometimes, I would be too tired to go anywhere after being on my feet all day hair styling. I could've been at work all day and he would still wait on me to come home, so I could go hang out with him. Since this was **unusual behavior**, I couldn't help but wonder if there was someone he was meeting up with the night of the mixer.

    The day had come, which also happened to be the day Taylor had a Christmas play at school. My mom and I drove separate from John, who had the mixer he wanted to attend, solo, immediately after. Deirdre and John's mom Brenda were there, sitting **together**.

CHAPTER 34

THE <u>DAY</u> OF MOM'S BRAIN SURGERY

One week later, the day before my mom's brain surgery, all of my siblings and I gathered at my mom's house. We had just found out less than 30 days prior, that she had a brain tumor. How we found out was suddenly, she stopped walking; I mean literally, STOPPED WALKING.

Red Cross had sent for my brother and sister-in-law, who were serving in the Army, to come for her brain surgery which was scheduled within four weeks of her finding out because of the 50/50 chance of her survival. It was critical for her to have surgery since the tumor was growing at such a rapid pace and there was a GREAT possibility that she could go into heart failure. When the doctor told us that, I heard him, but it didn't register. There was no doubt that my mom would not make it through that surgery. Although my mom and I were having our differences, she was STILL MY MOTHER and I still loved her and could not imagine her not being here with us.

My brothers, sister and the in-laws left to get food. John began to check his email on my brother's laptop. There was an email that John tried to hurry and scroll pass that read, "Cara Carter, Sends Big Kisses."

I stopped him and quietly asked, "John, who is Cara Carter and why is she sending kisses to you through your email?"

John tried to ignore me, so I asked again. John finally answered, "I'm not entertaining this." Then the argument started.

My mom asked, "What's wrong with you two? Why are you talking **at** each other quietly?"

Without a thought, I began to tell her about the email.

Then, she asked, "So, John, why won't you let Tori read the email?"

John and I exchanged a few more words, and then he walked out of the door. John began walking home before he called our friend to come and get him.

When my siblings returned, my mom asked my brother what he would've done in that situation. My brother answered, "If my wife is feeling insecure about something, it is my job as her husband, to make her feel secure again."

Baby Jaden and I left a few hours later.

When Jaden and I got home, I put her to bed. John and I had no words for one another, so I went to bed.

The next morning, December 15, at 5:30, the alarm sounded. John was due for work in an hour and I was due to take my mom in for pre-op. I got Jaden dressed and jumped in the shower. After I finished, John was still in the bathroom, so I grabbed Jaden and took John's cell phone and headed for the garage.

It was very cold that morning and I was wearing a blue jumpsuit. The top had a front pouch, where I placed John's cell phone. I was strapping Jaden in her car seat when I heard loud noises, as if someone was running down the stairs.

Suddenly, John bursts through the door YELLING, "GIVE ME MY PHONE, GIVE ME MY PHONE!!!"

Then, he pushed me back until I hit my head against the garage door. I began to fight back at this point. Finally, John pinned me against the garage door by my throat, pushing in with intense force. I remember feeling the ridges of the vertebrae in my neck as he pushed in until I could no longer inhale or exhale. I could NOT breathe and now feared for my life and the life I was carrying. I threw my hands up and looked him in the eyes. He looked at me and did a double-take, and dropped me. I began to gasp.

I handed him his phone. He snatched it then he yelled, "Don't nobody care that you're pregnant," and he walked back into the house.

After I caught my breath, I realized, that our seven-month-old daughter had been watching and hearing the whole thing.

I took Jaden out of the car and called my brother asking him to take mom to hospital because I "didn't feel good." After hanging up with him, I called the police.

John, attempting to have me arrested again, telling them that I had been arrested before and that I had started this. They looked him up in the system and noticed he had warrants and took him into custody.

CHAPTER 35

The CHURCH:
Confiding in the Co-Pastor

Fighting tears and snow, I finally made it to the hospital for my mom's brain surgery. I called Co-Pastor Mary. Hysterical and hurt I began to tell her what had happened a few hours prior as I cried and cried.

She jumped right in saying, "That was your fault for questioning him. Didn't I tell you that you had to be wise when you came down for prayer Sunday?

I answered, "Yes," as I cried attempting to tell her the rest of the story.

Then: "Wait a minute. Did I just hear you say that you were pregnant again?" she asked.

"Yes, and then…" I tried to continue.

"How did you let this happen? He wasn't doing anything for the one you two have already and now you are about to have another baby? He's made another deposit and now he can go on with his life but you are stuck with two babies," she responded in complete disappointment.

I was ashamed of myself by the time I had gotten off the phone with her. So ashamed, that I NO LONGER wanted to continue the pregnancy. With her words, the look of disappointment from my mom, and my husband telling me to have an abortion, the enemy attempted to convince me to make arrangements to end this *shame*. But I couldn't, I already loved the child that was growing inside of me.

After I pulled myself together, I finally made it into the hospital waiting room where my siblings were waiting. I smiled and pranced around, with Jaden, as if everything was okay. There were times when one of my siblings would take her. Those would be the times I would steal a moment to cry. I could not believe my husband had just pinned me against the garage door by my throat, *would this guy kill me? Does he really not want this baby? It doesn't matter. Whatever it is, we are a family and we are going to make this work.*

Each text message I received was a disappointing one because it wasn't John. I just knew that even if John didn't care for my mom, surely he would check on his daughter or attempt to come get her when he left work.

After finding out my mother's brain surgery was a success, Jaden and I went home. I let the garage up to find his car and things were gone. My stomach sank; I came home from my mom's brain surgery to find my husband gone. We had a seven-month-old daughter, and I was two months pregnant with our second child.

The

Separation

CHAPTER 36

PREGNANT, ALONE and HEART BROKEN

Even after the way he treated me, there were many nights I laid in bed crying until I fell asleep. Sometimes, I would awaken out of my sleep and cry all over again. I even began hearing voices in my head; words from my mom, Co-Pastor and his sister: "...people are going to look at you different." "He left you." "This is your fault." "He doesn't want you anymore now that you can't support him." "You make bad choices." "You are full of bad decisions." "Don't get pregnant by my brother!" "You married this type of man and now you want God to help you with your marriage." "I told you."

I began to go to sleep with Trinity Broadcast Network station turned up very loud to drown out those voices as they told me *life was not worth living.*

How many nights did I cry and think of calling and asking him to come home? I was pregnant and alone. We had a daughter together and there was another baby on the way that he had nothing to do with. Why would he not want us? I was hurt. I was devastated. I did things the right way. I waited to get married before having children, but that was no guarantee for a family. I later realized, *I married for selfish reasons, and then wanted God to fix it. But, God loves marriage; He called it "Good." So why is this happening to me? I wish he would just come home. We can work through this. We have children. What can I do to make me a better wife and person? What does he want to hear? What can I say that would work? What does he want? God fix it!!!*

I was sad, depressed, emotional and hurt. This was the pain I endured after being abandoned by the man who promised to love me.

CHAPTER 37

Although It Was A Bad Idea

Taylor and I had a SUPER relationship and EVERYONE knew it. I had received cards and compliments from John and his mother because of it. One year after John and I had been married, on Mother's Day, I received my first compliment via text message from Deirdre, "Happy Mother's Day and thank you for being so good to Taylor. She really loves you." That meant a lot because it's not often the parent of the child will compliment the step-parent. They may not say good things about the parent or step-parent but to KNOW the step-parent is great to their child and put pride aside and tell them, is nice. I didn't need it but the shock felt good.

While John and I were separated, I was three months pregnant when I received a phone call from Deirdre, "Hey, Tori, as you know, today is Taylor's birthday and I know you and John are separated, but Taylor has been BEGGING ME TO CALL YOU to come to her birthday party. She really wants her T.T. there. Can you **PLEASE** make it?"

I responded, "Probably not Deirdre. With all that's going on with John, his family and I. I don't think it would be a good idea. Tell her I will get her a birthday present though."

She put Taylor on the phone, "T.T., will you please, PLEASE come to my birthday party? I WANT YOU TO COME TO MY BIRTHDAY PARTY, I'M FIVE!!!"

Against everything I believed, Jaden and I went to the birthday party. Thirty minutes later, John showed up and had no words for me. Here we are, at Taylor's Birthday Party, and **MY HUSBAND** walks in the door and in front of all these people he interacted with everyone, BUT ME! It was hurtful but I kept a straight face. I spent an hour with them and left. A few hours later, Deirdre called apologizing to me for John's, **my husband's**, actions. She realized the awkward position that she had put me in. Taylor was happy so, I was okay.

When I was seven months pregnant, I called Deirdre to see if Taylor could come visit for a few hours to spend time with her little sister, Jaden, and me. Deirdre told me she could stay the night and she arranged for me to meet with her aunt who Taylor was with. Taylor had a great time with us.

CHAPTER 38

The Day Of EXCITEMENT, Or DISAPPOINTMENT

Finally, the day arrived that John and I were supposed to find out if we were having a baby girl or a baby boy. My mom and Jaden rode to the doctor's appointment with me; I was so excited knowing that John was going to meet us there too.

I had told John weeks before about the ultrasound appointment, so I hoped he would make it, as he told me he would. I sat in the lobby waiting for him. I tried to distract myself, but every time the door opened, I looked up with excitement, but sadly, no, it wasn't him. I kept waiting and waiting with anticipation until finally, the sonographer called me back. With every step and with a smile on my face, I still hoped and anticipated his arrival. *At any moment, he will walk through the door*, so I thought. I even thought, maybe when I walk into the room, he would be sitting inside with a smile on his face because he surprised me. But, no, the room only had ultrasound equipment, a chair and the table for me to lie on.

The sonographer began to prepare as I lay back on the table. I turned my face, as I felt my breathing getting shorter, my eyes welling up the tears. *Where is he?* I wondered, *he is my husband; this is an important moment and he should be here.* I couldn't really enjoy the ultrasound because I was too busy watching the door hoping that at any moment, it would open. It was a lonely feeling. *We are married, why is he tormenting me? My HUSBAND is choosing to embarrass me.* We had just been there the year prior; we knew the staff and the staff knew us. They knew I was a married woman, so where has my husband been during this pregnancy? The sonographer moved the sonogram around and said, "IT'S A GIRL." Knowing that John was going to be disappointed I asked, "Are you sure?" I began to shake my belly to get the baby to change positions. Maybe the sonographer would get a different reading.

After finding out the sex of the baby, I was okay but I knew John would not be. I thought about how I was going to break the news to him that he was about to have his third daughter. The sonographer handed me the sonograms and escorted me back to the lobby where I awaited the appointment with my doctor.

My mom and I were watching Jaden play when suddenly the door opened and John walked in. He walked to the counter asking where I was; I walked behind him and joked, "You don't have **any** boys in there???"

Shocked, he answered, "What are you talking about?" I handed him the sonogram and said, "It's a girl." He looked at the lady behind the counter and began to demand another sonogram. Finally I interrupted John, telling him, "John, you are an hour late. The baby is a girl," then I returned to my seat.

Sitting in silence the doctor finally called my name. While John and I set in the exam room in silence, mom brought baby Jaden in, "Here is y'alls baby," and went back to the lobby.

The doctor finally came in and checked the baby's heartbeat. He left out of the room. John said, "I will be back," and walked out of the room with baby Jaden. The doctor came back about five minutes later and examined me. He tried to wait for John to come back but finally told me that the pregnancy is going well and after reviewing the sonogram, everything looked good.

I walked back into the lobby and found only my mom and Jaden. I asked my mom, "Where is John?" She answered, "I guess he left. He brought Jaden to me and said he had things to do, and left." My stomach sank. I scheduled my following appointment and we left.

UH-OH!

I was twenty-seven weeks pregnant when I found out I had dilated to one and a half centimeters. The doctor warned me that it was too early to start dilating and that I needed to take it easy. There were three reasons why I could not "take it easy," I was a mother of a one-year-old, I was a working mother, and my husband walked out so I was a married woman having a single woman's experience. I didn't have the luxury to "take it easy."

By the time I was thirty-three weeks pregnant, I had dilated to three centimeters. The doctor mentioned putting me on bed rest. Again, I had three reasons: I still **had to** be a full-time mother to a twelve-month-old, and I **had to** keep the utilities on, so I **had to** work. He asked that I pretend to have a broken ankle. I agreed to play along.

I had back labor a few days later. I went to Labor and Delivery where I received the steroid shot. The steroid shot is given to women who go into early labor to help develop the baby's lungs, so he or she will have a better survival chance. I had to take one the first night then the other the next night. The nurse warned me that the shot was going to be painful and it was, excruciatingly painful.

CHAPTER 39

John, John, JOHN!

John came over for a visit. That day I had cooked salmon croquettes, cornbread, peas and mashed potatoes, so I offered him a plate to eat with Jaden. Jaden was sitting in his lap eating when the nice visit turned into an argument. Jaden seemed to start getting loud so I tried to monitor my actions by shutting down, hoping he'd eventually stop. It enraged him. He began yelling even more until suddenly Jaden climbed down from his lap, hit John's belly, and turned to me, hugging my legs with her head laid on my lap. I recognized that my baby did not like her daddy yelling at her mommy and wanted to protect me, so I leaned down and said,

"Baby, Mommy's okay. We're alright." I tried to assure her, patting her on the back.

Outraged, John yelled, "IS THAT WHAT SHE'S DOING? SHE'S GOING TO GET A SPANKING!!!"

I quietly responded, "John, you don't see that she doesn't like you yelling like that? She's reacting no differently than the time you were yelling at me in front of Taylor. The time she yelled for you to stop yelling at her 'T.T.'"

"WELL, YOU NEED TO TEACH HER NOT TO HIT ADULTS!!!" he yelled, then left slamming the door behind him.

Jaden cried for about an hour after that scene.

After that moment, John seemed to look at Jaden, not as his daughter, but an out-of-control one-year-old and his mission was to STRAIGHTEN HER OUT!

I had to distance myself from John by not taking his calls and not answering the door when he'd show up unannounced looking for a fight. Arguing was John's battlefield, he could yell in an argument one minute, then, invite me to watch a movie the next while I'm still distraught.

SLANDER

I came to church one Sunday, after being out of town and missing the previous Sunday, to find many church members asking me if John ever caught up with me.

One member pulled me to the side and whispered, "John came to church to get a chance to see his daughter because you are trying to keep her from him."

I figured Denise, my client, church member, and prayer warrior *knew* what was going on so I found her and asked, "What in the world is going on? John has been up here bashing me to everyone?"

She gave a slight smile and said in a mild tone, "Yeah, Tori, it was inappropriate."

To the ones that didn't know exactly what was going on, embarrassed, I began to explain, "My side."

I encountered the same problem with different people that I would run into outside the church -- John's mouth and his attempt to turn people against me. Even with that, the most I would do was defend myself but careful not to talk against him, just in case we got back together; again.

CHAPTER 40

The DAY ARRIVED

One day, after I finished my client's hair, mom and I went grocery shopping. By the time we had gotten in the car, "Wheeew!!" I sighed as a sharp pain shot through my lower abdominal area.

Mom looked over at me, "What's wrong?"

"I just felt a sharp pain shoot through my stomach," I answered. This pain was foreign to me because when I went into labor with the first baby, the pain was in my back. About 2-3 minutes later, "WHEEEW!!!" I gasped as I grabbed my belly.

Mom declared, "Call John and tell him to meet you at the hospital."

"No, mom, I have three relaxers next week and I need to make that money; so, just take me home and I will just try to stay off my feet," I calmly responded.

"NO! CALL JOHN BECAUSE I'M NOT GONNA BE ON THE SIDE OF THE ROAD DELIVERING A BABY!!!" mom retorted.

John was due to bring Jaden back to me within half an hour, so I called him so that he could meet mom instead. Plus I didn't want Jaden in the hospital room getting bored or busy while I lay up. John agreed and said he would come to the hospital afterward dropping Jaden at moms.

Mom dropped me off at the hospital. When I made it to Labor and Delivery, I walked through the doors very slowly, feeling a little bit uncomfortable. Two nurses were standing there talking but noticed me.

"Are you alright?" they questioned.

Holding my stomach, I calmly answered, "I think I'm in labor."

One rushed to get me a wheelchair, but I told her I was fine. The other braced my back and elbow and escorted me to a room.

A nurse, who remembered me from the week before, came in and asked, "You're in labor? What's happening? How are you feeling?"

She lubricated her gloves to examine me. I lifted and spread my legs then began telling her about the discomfort I was feeling. She then inserted two fingers deep inside me and pushed up.

"Ooooh!" I groaned in discomfort.

"Yep, you're in labor!" she acknowledged, "You are 5.5 centimeters dilated."

She asked if I wanted an epidural and I yelled, "YES!" as I immediately remembered thirteen months prior, shaking and nearly passing out from no medication until finally the pain was so great that I felt faint. I was 7.5 centimeters dilated. This time, I did not want to feel that type of pain again.

The moment when they put the baby belt around my belly, I heard my daughter's heart beating. It was comforting. I would lay there just watching the machine measure the intensity of the contractions while listening to her little heartbeat.

Finally, I exhaled; my husband walked through the door. Inside, I wanted to jump up, hug him, and thank him for coming but I didn't want to scare him or make him think that I assumed that he will come back to be with us; so, I just sort of smiled at him.

John sat down in the recliner, which was next to the bed I was lying in. Tick, tock, tick, tock. We watched a movie in silence. He made it clear that he was not there for me. This was not about me, or us.

The anesthesiologist came to administer the epidural. He recognized John and asked, "Don't you go to the Word of Life Church?"

John answered, "Yes."

They continued to talk while he prepped.

Then, he finally said those dreadful words, "I need you to lean forward and don't move. You're going to feel a pinch in your back and...."

Fear gripped me at the very thought of having a needle stuck into my back and not being able to flinch. I asked John if he would come and help brace my body so that I wouldn't move. I leaned over and put my head in his chest, gripped and held on to his triceps. In comfort, I stayed there careful not to move. He held my triceps. Wrapped in his chest and listening to his heartbeat reminded me of the first time we met; the many, many nights I fell asleep on his chest; and the pregnancy with our first child, how he cuddled me every night, falling asleep with his gripping pregnant belly.

For a brief moment I exhaled, it was the first time he touched me since the days before walking out on our daughter and I. I stayed in that position hoping it'd take the anesthesiologist a while, just so I could feel close to him again. So that he'd just hold me. I missed him. I missed him so much. My heart felt warm. Time stood still just like the day I met him. For a moment, I had my husband and he had me. He was there; I was holding onto him and he was holding me. We were *together*, even if it were only in my head.

After the epidural was administered, there were no more contractions or dilations. We found out that the epidural had stopped my labor. So, the next day, all day Sunday there was no activity. John was there all day. We NEVER said one word to each other, well, except when he would tell me to turn the television channel or the volume up or down. It was hurtful, and very disappointing. *This is my husband who is actually treating me this way, yet I want him here. What is wrong with me? Why doesn't he want me?* I thought.

Finally, on Monday morning, I had to wake John up because mom called and needing pampers for thirteen-month-old Jaden. John was pissed and suggested she wait a while because he was trying to get some sleep. I waited about ten minutes, then mom called me back to see if he had left. I woke him up again insisting he go and take mom pampers because she had ran out from having Jaden since Saturday. Angrily, John left.

The nurse came in and examined me. My labor had made no progress since the anesthetic was placed in my back.

"Your labor has not progressed since Saturday so we are going to have to send you home, Ms. Knight," Nurse Kelly said.

"Huh, although I'm six centimeters dilated?" I asked.

With a slight but sorrowful smile, she answered, "Yes, I'm sorry."

"No, NO! DON'T SEND ME HOME. PLEASE, DON'T SEND ME HOME! I CANNOT GO THROUGH THIS AGAIN. I CANNOT GO THROUGH THIS AGAIN!!! PLEASE!!!" I cried.

I began to cry uncontrollably as I recalled the past eight months to the last thirty-six hours: my husband in the room, but I was alone and LONELY. The pain of dejection was torture as my heart grieved inside. I could not bear going through this experience again. Of being so close to him, yet so far away, him being there; yet being absent. With the grieving heart, the pain, the humiliation, and the embarrassment, I felt like I was hemorrhaging inside. The stress of ALL OF IT! Absolutely not, *I cannot do this to my baby or myself.*

The nurse said, "Let me check you again."

I continued to sob uncontrollably, thinking that at any moment I was going to start vomiting if I didn't calm down. Then, Nurse Kelly said, "Tori, Tori, TORI, YOUR WATER JUST BROKE! YOUR WATER JUST BROKE!"

When I calmed down, I felt the warm water under my bottom. Oh, how relieved I was.

CHAPTER 41

Delivery and Drama

I called my mom and asked her if John had brought pampers over; and, I told her my water had just broken. She asked if was I going to call John and tell him, but out of fear of rejection, from both her and him, I told her, "No."

My mom, being a mother first, *knew* I wanted my husband with me for the delivery of our second child. She didn't tell me, but against everything she believed in, she put their differences aside and called to tell him that I was in labor.

Minutes later the nurse came in and told me that my husband was on the phone.

I answered, "Hello?"

"Tori, what's going on?" he inquired.

"Did you get pampers to Jaden?" I asked.

"Yeah," he answered.

"Okay, thank you," I responded as I prepared to hang up.

He stopped me, "WAIT, how are you doing'?"

Now, I knew that he knew. I answered, "Well, my water broke a little over ten minutes ago."

"Oh," he settled, "Well you're not going to have that baby no time soon, so --."

"But I'm already having contractions. The nurse just left out and said I'm dilating again. The baby's going to come soon!" I interrupted as I tried to control my emotions for wanting my husband to be there with me.

"Well, your water broke with Jaden and you didn't have her for like ten+ hours, so I'm going home to wash my nuts," he resolved, then hung up.

When he hung up, I held the phone for a few seconds trying to figure out how to call and convince **my husband** to come back for the birth of our new daughter. God, and my mom, **knew** I wanted him there. Well it would've been okay if someone that I knew was there, but there was no one. Not one person. Mom had my busy thirteen-month-old daughter, my sister was out of town getting married, my friends were at work, and my church family was at a Women's Conference. I finally hung up hoping that he'd be right about the baby coming later or *maybe he'd just surprise me and come back anyway*. Eventually, I grew tired of hearing the busy signal and I hung the phone up.

I laid there numb, watching the machine measure the intensity of my contractions while listening to my baby's heartbeat echo through the room. I rubbed my belly hoping that every time someone opened that door, it'd be my husband. Each disappointment of it not being him began to feel like a tearing in my heart. I felt empty.

About forty minutes later, I felt a thick heaviness in my groin area. It was a dull, weighty discomfort. I knew something was happening.

THE DIVORCE

I pushed the button, "NURSE, SEND SOMEONE! SOMETHING IS HAPPENING; SOMETHING IS WRONG!" I panicked.

Two nurses came in and one immediately examined me. She looked at the other nurse in the eyes and said, "The baby's head is here," then stood up and said to me, "Okay while we wait for your doctor this is what I need you to do…"

It seemed like an army of people began to come into the room. Every one of them introduced themselves as whatever their name were but half of them were part of the NICU, which was confusing. *Why is NICU here?* I thought. My nurses were prepping the room. I was fine and calm until an incubator rolled in. I began to panic and cry. Yes, everyone had introduced themselves, but *I* did not know them. There were **no** familiar faces that I knew personally. I thought: *Why are these people here? Are they going to try and take my baby? Who's going to hold my hand? Who's going to coach me? There's nobody here for me! What if they try and take my baby away. No one's here!*

I wanted to yell out, "I'm married you, guys. My husband is just not here, my sister is off getting married and my mom has my one-year-old toddler. I am loved; it's just my baby is early and my husband is not here yet!"

But, I couldn't talk at all. I suffered in silent humiliation, embarrassment and abandonment as it seemed that I was wearing a Scarlet Letter. I continued to sob. I could not help it as I searched the room again for a familiar face. Eventually, my doctor came in and I knew Nurse Kelly but they weren't my husband, family, or a friend.

Nurse Kelly came, stood beside me and held my hand. She rubbed my head and said, "Tori, look at me," I sadly looked over at her with tears falling and I began to sob, "Tori, calm down and breathe. Focus on your new baby. Focus on your new baby girl."

The others began asking me what's wrong; and telling me I should be happy. Nurse Kelly answered, "She's okay," but she knew I wasn't *and* she knew why.

Looking over my legs that were spread and in the air but covered with a sheet, Dr. Peters, with a big grin on his face asked, "Are you ready Mrs. Knight?

He was down in a quarterback position, so I nodded. Less than fifteen minutes later, they placed a five pound six ounce, crying baby girl on my chest. I cried and laughed with joy because immediately, the atmosphere of the room changed when she let out that loud, "WAAA, WAAA!" Her lungs were okay and the NICU team smiled and congratulated me as they rolled the equipment out of the room. I was so HAPPY. My baby was healthy; my heart was warm. Everything was WONDERFUL.

Nurse Kelly informed me that if she would have been born **just one day earlier**, they would have taken her because any baby born under thirty-five weeks is automatically taken into the NICU.

You are talking about feeling the glory and praising God. *Lord, you didn't allow her to come early because you knew my heart wouldn't have been able to bear them taking my baby away. I went into labor early, but it stopped suddenly. I didn't understand why but then, the day I turned thirty-five weeks, right when they came in to send me home, You allowed a healthy baby girl to come. You are AWESOME!*

To have gone through hell in my pregnancy just for them to take her from me, I don't know what the outcome would've been. I was so grateful. Gratefulness just filled my heart because "joy comes in the morning" and it did.

The nurses cleaned Baby Aaron up after weighing her. Maybe five minutes after Aaron was born, and while my doctor and nurses were working on getting the placenta, the room was still filled with joy and peace.

AAAAAAND then 5,4,3,2...

John bursts through the doors yelling, "WHY YOU DIDN'T CALL ME? WHY YOU DIDN'T TELL ME?"

Embarrassed, I yelled back, "I DID TELL YOU, YOU SAID YOU HAD TO GO WASH YOUR NUTS!!!"

John looked over and saw minutes old Baby Aaron who was being cleaned up. Upon finishing, I noticed that he didn't ask to hold her, he only took pictures.

My mom came to the hospital about forty-five minutes after my delivery to introduce Jaden to her new baby sister.

John stood up and said he was going to Grandy's to get something to eat and asked if anybody wanted anything. Mom, unaware that John missed Aaron's birth, couldn't decide so she and Jaden rode with him.

Mom called when they had arrived and asked what I wanted.

Excited to finally be able to eat, I told her, "A FISH DINNER!"

She told John, who I heard in the background say, "Naw, the hospital can feed her!"

I heard the thunder roll and saw the dark cloud hover over the earth because I **know** my mom.

To make sure she didn't put John in a chokehold, I said, "OH, MOM, that's okay; I have the menu and I can eat whatever I want here."

She calmly said, "Okay, Tori. We'll be back shortly."

Hearing the calmness in her voice, I panicked, "Mom, I believe they have fish here; I will order something now!"

Mom muttered, "Mmm-hmm," and hung up.

I tried to call back, but she wouldn't answer. I laid there nervously twirling my toes. Then, I turned on the news thinking, *OH MY GOD, please don't make the afternoon news mom! Please don't! Answer the phone mom! Remember that Jaden is with you guys. Lord, PLEASE don't let my mom hurt him!*

Eventually, they came back with food. I don't know what happened, but mom walked up to me with a bag and said, "Here you go. John bought you some fish."

I looked at her, then I looked over at him who was sitting down opening his eating utensil packages and condiments. I thanked him. He never looked up, he just said, "Yeah," and began to eat. She looked at him in disgust, then looked me and rolled her eyes.

Things were back to normal, they couldn't be in the same room at the same time. Between the food incident at Grandy's and obviously finding out NO ONE, including MY HUSBAND, whom she had called, was there for the Aaron's delivery, my obviously annoyed mom grabbed her bag of food, kissed Jaden, and prepared to leave.

I asked John if was taking Jaden with him, he said, "I can take her for a few hours, but I have to work tonight."

Mom said, "Tori, I can just take her now."

I looked at John, who said nothing.

John held Aaron for a few minutes then said he had something to do, and he left.

John called me a few hours later, "You need me up there for anything?"

I replied, "No, we're okay."

He responded with an attitude, "Okay then!" then he hung up.

CHAPTER 42

DRAMA BEFORE DISCHARGED

The next day, mom and Jaden came to the hospital to for a visit. The hospital staff had brought in a round table, a white table cloth, salad, mashed potatoes, asparagus, steak, lobster, pie and cranberry juice for the happy couple, just as they had done last year.

Aware that the dinner is for the happy couple, I asked my mom, "Are you ready to eat?"

Mom, Jaden and I ate well while Baby Aaron laid in the hospital baby bed. About an hour later, after everything was cleaned up, John walked through the door. Mom, not being able stomach him, especially when she found out he missed the birth, immediately got up to leave; but first she wanted to make sure that John was going to take Jaden for a while so that she could have a break. He agreed.

After she left, John asked me, "So, when are we going to eat steak and lobster?"

With a slight inside tickle, I answered, "Mom and I already ate it."

He sat down and began to play with Jaden having nothing to do with Aaron.

The birth certificate employee came in and went over all the information and asked if it was correct.

I looked at John and asked, "John, is all the information correct?"

He looked at the documents while holding Jaden and said, "Nah, take my name off that birth certificate because that baby ain't mine."

After the lady left, I told John to get out and take Jaden to my mom's after his visit with her. Then, I walked my newborn to the nurse station and told them to keep her. I went back to my room and cried. I could not hold it any longer. I cried and cried. I was glad that I was at the end of the hall because I was unable to stop and I didn't want to disturb the other mothers. This cry was from my belly. It was coming from my soul. I finally took two hydrocodone pills and cried myself to sleep.

The following day, my original postpartum nurse came in from being absent for three days. I looked at her, and she stared at me as if she was pissed.

"You know what's going on, don't you?" I asked.

She answered, "Yes, WE ALL knew from the moment he came out of the delivery room and asked where he could get a paternity test because 'that baby' wasn't his. Enough, if he comes back up here, we're going to call security and have him escorted off the premises."

I nodded in agreement, turned over and cried. I was so embarrassed. I could not figure out why my husband, was tormenting me.

I called my sister-in-law and gave her the new information about John's request for paternity immediately after Baby Aaron's arrival. Shocking to me, she did not seem shocked. She tried to find comforting words while attempting to hide the anger for having already heard the information that I had just found out.

After that conversation, I cried again. I had cried so much that eventually my body felt as if I had been chained behind a speeding car that had been driving for miles. I was physically and emotionally exhausted.

CHAPTER 43

"Mama's Baby, Daddy's Maybe"

I could NOT understand why he was doing this to me, but later it made sense. I found out his mother had altered the story she told me about how she named John. She named him after her boss because she was having an affair with him. Both of them were married and when she had John, she left her husband. Not only did she have an affair, but her mother also had an affair and a child while she was still married to her husband. That generational curse and the sins of his mother and grandmother were tormenting John, therefore they tormented our marriage. He didn't trust me because he didn't trust women.

I kept begging for my husband to come back home but it seemed the more I begged, the more he enjoyed it and stayed away. Finally, at the child support review, I walked in late and exhausted with my fourteen-day-old baby.

Obviously they had already been chatting so when I walked in the door, holding Aaron in the carrier, she rudely said to me, "Mrs. Knight, Mr. Knight has concerns for whether your two children are his and wants to have both of them DNA tested. Can you be there in an hour?"

"Yes," I answered as I wondered what he told her for her to have that attitude towards me.

I felt sick because he is actually going to carry this game out trying to please his mom. *Really???* After the case worker left out to get the hospital's address; I sat down. Silence... then here we go.

I quietly said to him, "John, I have found an attorney that will handle our divorce for $500. You and I can go in half." (This was **not** the reaction I was expecting).

He said, "Alright then." Then, suddenly he reacts, "DIVORCE! YOU WANT A DIVORCE?"

"Uhh, I mean clearly we are not getting back together. Right?" I asked.

Shaking his head, "You don't get it! YOU JUST DON'T GET IT, DO YOU?"

Shocked, I responded, "Get what? We are sitting here in at the ATTORNEY GENERAL'S OFFICE for child support; AND NOW, you think I'm cheating!"

"CHEATING???" he asked.

Almost in a head spin I answered, "JOHN, we are on our way to have the babies DNA TESTED!!!"

The caseworker came back in the room and gave us the address. We parted ways.

By the time I had gotten to my car, I called my mom and told her to bring Jaden to the hospital because John was having *both* of the girls DNA tested. She went off but met me at the hospital with Jaden.

How embarrassing. I am at the DNA clinic as Mrs. Knight because Mr. Knight, MY HUSBAND, is having our children tested. How humiliating. I was his WIFE. I was his wife who had NEVER stepped out on him, who had never even been caught with another man, even when we had episodes every month about women. I NEVER stepped out! The best he had on me were phone calls. Why? Because in my immaturity, I decided to talk on the phone to guys since he was doing it. He would understand how it felt, but one of his flimsy excuses was, "Well, Deirdre is my daughter's mother, so I have to talk to her often." But he had no words about the other women.

I thought, *he never respects our agreement regarding talking on the phone to the opposite sex; I have to hear from his baby's mama that he still be calling her. Maybe he will see how it feels.* Nothing got by him anyway because he checked my cell phone calls and texts everyday.

A few days later, my doorbell rang. I looked out and became excited because it was him. My heart began to flutter as my thoughts went wild, *Lord, please let it be that he's coming home. Our little discussion the other day has him thinking and now he wants to come home and be with his family.* I got myself together and answered the door.

He immediately began, "Tori, you seriously want a divorce?" I told him I didn't, but he if he walked out and didn't come back, I couldn't be a part of his little game anymore. Sad to say, we ended up talking in circles, then, he left. Nothing was accomplished. My heart was broken. *What can I do to get this man to come home? How do I make this pain go away? I just want my husband back. I will do anything for him to just come back home. We can work this out.* I cried myself to sleep. Again!

A month later, we went back to the Attorney General's office. He asked to hold our two-month-old daughter as we waited in the lobby for our names to be called. He talked "Daddy" talk to her, which let me know, that he knew in his heart that she was his. Although I kept up the façade, my heart melted and I hoped his was melting, too.

Finally, we were called back to an office. This was a different case worker and he immediately began telling John how much he owed for child support and in back child support.

John, STILL HOLDING our small baby, stopped him and said, "Wait, have you got the test results? I don't even know if they mine!" My heart sank again as if I had never heard that before.

The case worker paused, then said, handing us the DNA result copies, "They're both yours. Anyway..."

John should've felt two-inches tall because that young man never flinched as if he'd seen men like John a thousand times and they all disgust him. The case worker told John how much back child support he owed for our first child adding up to close to $3,000. He then figured out the child support that he would owe monthly for our two children which came out to be $552 per month.

John went off, "DO YOU SEE THAT I HAVE ANOTHER CHILD BESIDES THESE TWO? THAT'S GOING TO TAKE CLOSE TO A THOUSAND DOLLARS A MONTH FOR ALL OF THEM. THAT'S TOO HIGH! HOW YOU COME UP WITH THAT? HOW AM I SUPPOSED TO LIVE? I DON'T MAKE THAT MUCH..."

Now at this point, our nursing baby was eight-weeks-old and John's weekend was coming up. As the case worker advised, I visited John's apartment to be sure it was child-proof and toddler-friendly. John had a two-bedroom townhome in not one of the best areas but I had never heard of any drive-by shootings. In one empty room, HE HAD AN OLD BABY CRIB THAT HAD TO HAVE BEEN FOUND BY A DUMPSTER. I had never seen a baby crib that had wide bars, no legs, and a cushion that was about one-inch thin. If our daughter would've been crawling, she could've gotten her head caught in the wide bars (and, well, you know the rest). Since it was ON THE FLOOR, there was a great possibility that an insect could've gotten into her mouth or a spider could've bitten her. Also, there was no crib bedding on that cushion. There were a few things that I didn't agree with that I couldn't ignore.

I called John and tried to reason with him.

"John, you know Aaron is nursing and Jaden doesn't know you yet. Do you mind spending the day with them but bring them back home at night? It would be good if we can graduate with the times until you all really get to know each other."

"NAW!" he snapped back," They'll be alright!

I pleaded, "John, Aaron is nursing every two hours."

"So! You don't produce enough milk. Plus, I got milk over here anyway!" he said.

"What kind of formula do you have?" I asked.

"I don't know! The one with the blue top!" he said with an attitude.

"Oh, my God, Powder?" I asked in shock.

"Yeah, Tori!" he said frustrated.

"JOHN, I SPECIFICALLY TOLD YOU SHE CAN NOT DRINK REGULAR OR POWDERED MILK. SHE HAS GASTRO ESOPHAGEAL REFLUX AND SUPPOSED TO ONLY DRINK BREAST MILK AND LIQUID ALIMENTUM. AND, SHE TAKES MEDICATION FOR IT. THAT MILK IS GOING TO MAKE HER SICK!" I explained.

"Well, I already bought it. She'll be alright. Have them ready. I'll see you Friday," he demanded and hung up.

I went to the Attorney General's office and told them my concern. I asked if we could get the times changed for no overnight stays until the children were a little older and they all were better acquainted. He advised me to take that matter to court, so I dropped the child support case until I could do that.

That decision to make was a hurtful one because this would delay time for John getting to know and bond with his daughters. I did not have my dad in my life so I determined that my daughters would have theirs. Plus, I was so looking forward to having some time to sleep. Having a one-year-old and a nursing eight-week-old…was exhausting, EXHAUSTING! I really needed the break; I was tired.

On Friday, my brother sent a text, "John and some white guy just left here looking for you. I told him where you work and they are on their way up there. John has a camera around his neck."

I read the text to my mom who immediately went off, "WAIT A MINUTE, DID YOU SAY JOHN WAS AT MY HOUSE? MY HOUSE!!! OH, NO! AND NOW HE'S ON HIS WAY UP HERE?

OKAY, I WILL BE RIGHT IN THE PARKING LOT WAITING FOR HIM! YOU STAY IN HERE!!!"

Although I was with a client, I continued to watch for John out of safety concerns (for him). Sure enough, he came to the salon with a camera around his neck and a white guy; they both got out.

They walked up and John said, "Tori, I'm here to pick up my kids."

My mom jumped in front of me. He could only address me by going **through** her, "WHAT KIDS? THOSE KIDS YOU SAID AREN'T YOURS?"

"Tori, I'm here to pick up my kids," he said remaining calm.

I tried to respond but mom was already on 10, "JOHN, YOU HAD THESE KIDS TESTED AND NOW THEY YOURS!!!" Then, she turned to the white guy and yelled, "WHO ARE YOU!!!"

John said, "This is Tim, my co-worker," and once again, this time stepping to the side to get full eye contact with me, he demanded, "WHERE ARE MY KIDS, TORI?"

I jumped in before my mom took my turn and said, "John, I called you and told you that I dropped the case and that we will go before a judge to come up with a reasonable time since you weren't willing to work something out, so you will not be getting them this weekend," then I turned around and walked back in to the building.

I could hear my mom yelling and following them back to John's car. They got in and let the windows down. Shocked, my mom yelled, "YOU DON'T HAVE AIR?? (Yes, I had forgotten to tell her that part) YOU MUST BE OUT OF YOUR MIND IF YOU

THOUGHT WE WERE GOING TO LET YOU TAKE AN EIGHT-WEEK-OLD BABY WITH YOU FOR AN ENTIRE WEEKEND FIRST OF ALL. SECOND, YOU THOUGHT YOU WERE GOING TO DRIVE FORTY-FIVE MINUTES TO YOUR MOTHER'S HOUSE IN 108 DEGREE WEATHER. AND, SINCE YOU DON'T HAVE AIR CONDITIONING, ALL THE AIR WOULD BE GOING BACK ON THEM GIVING THE BABY COLIC! YOU MUST BE OUT OF YOUR MIND!!!"

When I walked into the building, I broke down. I just could not believe I was going through this.

My mom came back in still on level 10, "TORI, DID YOU KNOW HE DIDN'T HAVE AIR?? HE MUST BE CRAZY!!!"

Right at that moment, my neighbor called me, "Tori, the police and John were at your house about thirty minutes or so, ago and..."

CHAPTER 44

The Church: Again

I had not been in church since Co-Pastor had judged and rebuked me. I had finally gotten the nerve to go back for I loved my church family and I missed them.

After service was over, Co-Pastor was standing by the exit doors hugging members as they left. When my turn came, I pulled the blanket off two-month-old Aaron and pointed to her with happiness, "Hi, Pastor, here is the baby."

She leaned in and said, "She's a pretty baby. She looks just like the other one," pointing to one-year-old Jaden sitting in front of the stroller.

I joked, "Well, according to the DNA tests, they're both his."

She answered, "He's crazy. But so are you because this second baby didn't have to happen."

I walked out the doors, not looking back.

I called my mom crying, telling her what Pastor had said.

She replied, "Oh, she just said what everyone else was thinking."

What stabbed me in my Heart

I called another lady minister (close friend to the Pastors) and told her what I had just heard from "someone in the church."

She said, "Tori, don't listen to that. That's not GOD! Tori, tell Pastor Mary your story. She will be able to give you her testimony about how Pastor Tony left her and their two little sons for an entire year. The older ladies of the church encouraged her on how to believe GOD for her marriage and to prepare their home DAILY as if she were **expecting** him to come home."

Her words began to fade as I reflected, in shock, back on the conversation I had had with her less than a twenty-four hours ago. I never told her about my conversation with the pastor because *surely* she was talking about someone else. Surely!

I later talked to my mentor, Ms. Beverly, about what had happened that morning and how I had called a Pastor to talk to her for comfort and how she ended up judging and condemning me.

She encouraged me with the same story the other minister shared, "You should talk to Pastor Mary; Pastor Tony left…"

Her words began to fade as I reflected because then I *knew* that it really was her. When she finished telling me Pastor Tony and Pastor Mary's testimony, I got enough nerve and said, "It was Pastor Mary that condemned me."

THE

DIVORCE

CHAPTER 45

Filing for Divorce

My baby was going on three-months-old when I finally realized the madness needed to stop. The police had either been to my house or called on me at least twenty-five times by John. I had no support for the children, even after the paternity results had come back.

Because I was John's wife, he felt it was okay to fight and make-up with me. He found it amusing to dangle the carrot before the horse by dropping by anytime he wanted entertainment, and giving me hope that we were going to make our marriage work and be a family again. The effect the bickering was having on not only my babies, but Taylor, too. I knew I had to do something.

The ball was in his court and he knew it. I felt that I had no choice but to file for the divorce because I had to end this game of limbo. I knew one of two things would happen: we would get back together (even in dysfunction) or the divorce would go through. Either way, it was going to hurt.

My mom's church member, who had just gone through a divorce, had told me to contact Tammy, her church member who worked for legal aid to handle my divorce since I had no money. I applied and was accepted. A week later, I made the appointment.

My mom and I walked in with one-year-old Jaden and three-month-old Aaron. It was the moment, *that* moment. Before Tammy called me into her office, I prayed, "Heavenly Father, YOU know

THE DIVORCE

all and YOU see all. I don't want to divorce my husband, but he left me and our children. Even has accused me of infidelity. I don't want this divorce, LORD. YOU CAN STOP THIS IF IT'S YOUR WILL. I don't want a divorce and I am willing to do anything You want me to do to save my marriage. I have prayed, cried, gone to jail, have been humiliated, but if it's Your Will, I will stay in this marriage."

Tammy had called me in and we began the paper work. I knew when I made the appointment with Tammy that I didn't want a divorce, but I felt John had abandoned us and I was going crazy.

I was tough on the outside but dying on the inside. I cried every night. I wanted my husband back, but I couldn't tell ANYONE, but God.

CHAPTER 46

GUESS WHO CAME TO COURT

Our first court date had arrived. There was a murder trial and they needed more space so our hearing was moved to a smaller courtroom. I exited the elevator. As I strolled the lobby looking for the courtroom, I found a very familiar face talking on the phone, Deirdre.

Without hesitation, I walked passed her and spoke, "Hi, Deirdre!"

I was shocked to see her but thought nothing more of it because I had just spoken with her a few months ago and we had a pretty cool mother-to-mother relationship. But, I was very curious as to why she would be all the way in Collin County Courthouse. I really tried to make sense of this coincidence as I walked into the courtroom. John saw me and walked out. A few minutes later, both Deirdre and John walked in the courtroom and sat down together, two rows in front of me.

I sat there in shock. I sent my mom, mother- and sisters-in-laws, my friend, and my pastors a text message, "John's daughter's mom, Deirdre, is here with John!"

I couldn't help but think *I cannot believe Deirdre is here. I have taken great care of her daughter. I have paid child support. I bought clothes. I took her to work with me. I BONDED with her to the point where her relationship with me was deeper than her and John's. Deirdre and Taylor called and begged me to come to*

Taylor's birthday party because she wanted her T.T. there; I attended **knowing** I was walking into the Lion's Den with Deirdre, our children's father, my estranged husband, and his sister. I JUST KEPT TAYLOR AT MY HOUSE A FEW MONTHS AGO!

Because Deirdre was Taylor's mom I thought we could still be amicable because our daughters were sisters. Plus, we had the same experiences with the same man, **and his mother**. Wow, how naïve was I?

Maybe fifteen minutes after Deirdre and John had sat down she came and asked if she could speak with me outside, "I just wanted you to know, I'm not on John's side, I'm not on your side; I'm just here to say that he's a good father and that Taylor adores her dad. I do want to apologize to you because I have said some things about you to John and his mother. Also, Tori, it's so important for children to have their fathers in their lives for them to be stable. I kept jumping in and out of relationships; and I **had** my father in my life..."

After that, anything she said did not matter as my mind began to wander, *This entire time I've known you, John has been "no good, a dead beat, stupid, unstable..." and now that we are getting a divorce he's a "good father?" Now, "It's so important for children to have their fathers in their lives. I kept jumping in and out of relationships; and I **had** my father in my life." So your father was **in** your life, and according to John, Brenda **and you,** you **still** jumped in and out of relationships? AND...YOU'RE ADVISING ME?!? And, testifying for him. Wow, they warned me.*

A few seconds later my attorney called me into a side room to discuss my concerns and requests regarding visitations, child support, insurance and child care to see if we could work something out with John, before we faced the judge. I was okay with attempting to work with John but Deirdre had nothing to do with this and she is not to come back here. She agreed and called John in announcing, that she only needed him.

About twenty minutes into our attempt at negotiation, Deirdre walked in. My attorney stopped her and informed her that we'd be out shortly. Deirdre walked back into the lobby and John walked out after her. We had gone back-and-forth but sadly, John would not compromise anything; therefore, we didn't come to an agreement.

My attorney and I finished discussing the requests that we would bring before the judge. I walked into the lobby to find John and Deirdre sitting on the bench talking. I sat on the other side of the bench until it was time to be called in. I don't remember feeling so uncomfortable. The very thought of how Taylor maybe feeling was sickening. I could only imagine what disparaging remarks she was hearing about and had she been turned against me. We ended up having to wait until after lunch to go before the judge.

My attorney friend sent me a message advising me to tell my attorney to ask Deirdre to recall the many times she called regarding the time Taylor was being bounced around to John's different relatives; the time when Taylor had come back home with a rash because John continued to use soap that he knew caused her to have allergic reactions; the time she asked for John to be monitored since he had a habit of talking bad about her in front of Taylor and turning Taylor against her.

After lunch, it was our turn. John came pro se and I was represented by an attorney. I don't know what happened to Deirdre because she was not there, but the person who was there -- MY MOM! YES, SITTING ONE ROW BEHIND ME.

AND 5, 4, 3, 2

John took full advantage of representing himself to the female judge, Judge Patterson, by lying, crying, and putting on a show:

"She's bitter because she wants me back! She wasn't paying her bills. She would put me out then lights and stuff would get cut off and I would have to come back and catch her up on all of her bills. Finally, I left her Your Honor," he began to cry (Violins were playing in the background). "I had to leave her because she kept putting her hands on me. She was beating me and hitting me Your Honor and she was abusing my other daughter. She even went to jail for abuse. I stayed with her because I know she has some issues, but when she began to abuse my daughter I had to leave her, and my kids. Now, she's trying to keep me away from them because she is bitter. SHE'S KEEPING ME AWAY FROM MY KIDS YOUR HONOR!!!"

Then, he flopped down into the seat and began to sob uncontrollably, making his shoulders jump up and down.

Judge Patterson looked at John and sympathetically asked, "Mr. Knight, do you need a minute?"

John nodded his head as he pretended to get himself together; adding, "Your Honor, I apologize. It just hurts me to see her use my kids to hurt me. She can be mean and vindictive and try to turn people against me. Now, she's trying to get me to pay child support AND daycare after all this time. She would call me and tell me the children needed something, then she would go buy herself something. She is even abusing the system because she is doing hair out of her home, but I don't think she is reporting it to the IRS. She gets food stamps but she would call me and tell me that they didn't have food cause she knew I would come and bring her money so that my children could eat." Sobbing again, "Now her and her mother won't let me see them at all. They just want to take all my money and not let me see my children!!!"

"Mr. Knight," Judge Patterson compassionately asked the emotional John, "Mr. Knight, how do you eat?"

John sadly answered, "Your Honor, I just eat when I can."

That did it! Suddenly, the bailiff stood up. I already knew why. I saw the dark cloud hover the earth as I prayed that my mom would not jump over that little door. My mom had jumped to her feet.

Judge Patterson said, "Ms. Lynn, if you cannot control yourself then," Mom cut her off, "YOUR HONOR, HE IS SITTING OVER THERE LYING; JOHN DON'T HAVE ANY MONEY!"

The judge continued, "Well, if you cannot control yourself then you will have to leave."

"WELL, LET ME LEAVE THEN BECAUSE HE IS LYING..." mom continued to rant as she walked towards the doors. Now with the bailiff behind her, she yelled, "WHO'S GOING TO PROTECT THE CHILDREN???"

After mom left, I turned to the judge and begged for her mercy, "Your Honor, she's had a brain tumor, PLEASE…" The judge nodded and we kept going.

The utter betrayal is what stabbed me in my heart: to have been given cards by his mother, calls, and text messages from Taylor's mother and John, about being such a good step-mother to Taylor for taking her to work with me, to have watching kid movies together, to have taught her to ride her bike, to teaching her to spell her name, and other things. One of the times John and I had reconciled we had gone to pick Taylor up for our weekend visit. When she saw me in the car, four-year-old Taylor ran into me shouting, "T.T., T.T., I MISSED YOU T.T.!" I sat in the back seat with her and we held hands. There was even a time when Taylor had an ear infection and Deirdre allowed her to come with us anyway because she KNEW I would take care of her.

Needless to say, the judge favored John.

CHAPTER 47

Meet Our Daughters

The judge set John's visitation schedule: two hours – 6:00 p.m. to 8:00 p.m. every Thursday and 7:00 a.m. to 5:00 p.m. every other Saturday and Sunday. She went a step further and gave him every Tuesday and every Saturday; extra days that he DID NOT request.

Now, our first visitation meeting for the girls and his first time seeing our four-month-old daughter since the paternity test results, was on a Thursday at McDonald's.

He had called a few hours before and asked, "Tori, for our first meeting, would you make it just me, you and the girls? I know it's their first time meeting with me and I want them to feel comfortable with just me, you and them."

I agreed to it. I called my mom and told her about his request. Her response was, "WHAT? AFTER WHAT HE JUST DID IN COURT, NOW HE WANTS TO PLAY FAMILY! NOW, I'M GOING TO MAKE SURE I'M THERE. HE DOESN'T CALL SHOTS!!!"

We *all* met at McDonald's that evening. Mom was sitting a few tables away.

When he came in, I said, "Jaden, give your daddy a hug."

Then, I invited him to sit down and meet his new baby girl. I pulled the sheet from over the car seat; she looked up at him and smiled. I took Aaron out of her car seat and placed her in John's arms while Jaden played beside him on the bench. When I returned from buying Jaden's fries he was trying to take pictures of himself with the girls. I asked if he wanted me to take a picture of all three of them. He said, yes.

My mom called me to the table where she was sitting and went left, "YOU OVER THERE TAKING PICTURES? THIS MAN HAS LEFT YOU AND NOW HE WANTS TO TAKE AND POST PICTURES LIKE HE'D BEEN THERE THE WHOLE TIME? HE HAS NOT SUPPORTED THEM AT ALL, SAID THEY WEREN'T HIS, AND NOW, HE EMBARRASSED YOU IN COURT! NOW, YALL ARE OVER THERE TAKING PICTURES???"

After I thought about it, I was pissed all over again. I walked back to him and said, "I will see you at 8 o'clock," and then, I walked out the door.

When I returned, at 8:00 p.m., Jaden was playing in the Playland and Aaron was asleep in her car seat. All was well.

CHAPTER 48

How Did I Get Here

Our final court date has arrived. I sat in the courthouse lobby; I couldn't help but wonder *How did I get here? I waited to get married before having children. I cooked, I cleaned, and I was a good mother to Taylor. I supported my husband. We had so much sex that at one point he told me, "Baby you are wearing me out. I was faithful and committed to my husband and my marriage. I faithfully went to church and believed God would heal my marriage. HOW DID I GET HERE?* Then I realized…

I chose John out of my pain and current circumstances. **I made the choice** to marry John with the waving **RED FLAGS** and the **FLASHING WARNING** signs. I did NOT ignore them, I simply collected them believing I could work with them and make a difference and prove everybody wrong. I needed him; well, maybe not **him** but I needed the love, affirmation and acceptance that he gave me. I'd always felt that I was never enough.

The pain I was dealing with was from my past. The Stepfathers: one was an alcoholic, the other pinned me against a closet door and beat me with a wave brush. My dad: he is an unstable drug addict who is abusive to women. He has never laid a finger on me and I have never questioned his unconditional love for me even in his absence. The Jehovah's Witness organization: my mom and stepdad were part of the organization, so I had a lot of bible knowledge but no love. I was taught religion but not relationship. I **did not** know that God loved me. My mom had no self-love because of her complexion therefore she could not love us.

John admired and complimented me daily. He was excited about me and wanted to show me off to the world. I needed an inner healing and to be delivered from people pleasing. If I *knew* of God's Unconditional Love and Acceptance, I wouldn't have needed mans. I walked around, thinking I had it all together until that moment.

Unrealistic Expectations

"I didn't marry him because he was not ready," Deirdre said in an early conversation. She was right; surely he wasn't ready to be a husband because at that point, he was not yet a man. I owe him an apology for **unrealistic expectations**. I tried to make him be something he was not. I put him in a role and expected him to play it without any training, experience or model. How unfair.

I honestly thought that my showing John how to manage money, pay bills and pay them on time, the advantages of having good credit, and having favor with GOD and man it would change his outlook on life and he would make better decisions.

I had grown to love John; he had become my best friend and I wanted to make a difference. He was a man no different from the man my mom had chosen to be my father; nor was he any different from the man my grandmother had chosen to be my mom's father. So honestly, John not having it together didn't really seem all that bad.

By this time my relationship with my mom had become extremely arduous. Although her delivery was wrong, I understand that her heart was in the right place as she attempted to shield me from the heartache that she saw coming. She was so combative. I felt that she was trying to control the decisions I made. She didn't want me to take in my paternal brother because he was a troubled eleven-year-old; but, he was my brother and I had to take him and try and make a difference. She was afraid that he'd take my car, or put my house on fire as he has someone else car and house. Sure enough I did make a difference. He got saved. And, I didn't have near the problems that his maternal side had with him. I had regular teen troubles with him. Then, John. No he did not have what I had or better. Again, I felt I could make a difference. My mom was a foster parent to over fifty foster children; I saw many lives changed. Yes, she tried to protect me but her delivery, I felt had backed me into a corner. At age twenty-nine, was I rebelling? Do adults rebel? The Ephesians 6:1 says that children must obey their parents. Was I disobedient? Am I being punished? Does that scripture still apply to me in my adult years???

I lost my faith in God because I could not find Him in all of the confusion. The enemy was very crafty at keeping me so focused on the mess I was in by continually reminding me of my faults through my thoughts, my situation, and people. I had forgotten how to focus on the Creator and buried my pain in my soul. My heart was torn to pieces. I felt like I had been hit with the bat of life, and shattered pieces of me went with the wind. I didn't trust myself, my friends, or my God. I felt forsaken; I couldn't see the Potter.

Since then, I have forgiven myself for the mistakes that I made that had gotten me to this place. I've always had the gift of compassion and I have always been in a position where I was able to help or bless people. Yes, sometimes it gets abused. I have always had a forgiving heart but now I have learned the **power** of forgiveness, decisions, and cause and effect. I learned that Words **DO** hurt! Although we continue to keep pushing, when hurtful words come from those you love, it has its way of lurking into your subconscious. If you continue to be around those people who are hurting you, eventually, the hurt will come to the forefront and MANIFEST itself in one way or another. I have learned that I can't change people, especially grown people.

There is only ONE that can change one, but more importantly, the only ONE that I **needed** the whole time was GOD.

Wow, what a lesson.

CHAPTER 49

FINALLY, IT'S OVER!

Finally, we were before Judge Patterson. It seemed that John continued to win favor in the eyes of the court although I presented the court with John's proof of instability, emails from his sister, texts, proof of phone calls, inconsistent visits on Saturdays, late pickups, and early drop offs. I also had three witnesses: my mom, my sister and my client. I also submitted countless letters from friends and (his) family; still she continued to favor him. Judge Patterson caught John in a lie when he claimed my mom had hit him. She totally eradicated his back child support, awarded him the truck that *my* business bought, and continued to allow him to have extra Tuesdays that he did not ask for (which totally worked against him later). She told us that when Jaden turned three, she would begin staying overnight.

After all of that, the judge finally granted our divorce declaring, "Now that the divorce is over, the fighting should die down." She was right. The **fighting** died down. But... the very next weekend the **battles**...

BEGAN!

COMING SOON....

TABOO

Let's Talk about SEX!

Biography

Tori Lynn is an author and motivational speaker dedicated to speaking to men and women who are facing, going or has gone through a divorce or hardship. Tori obtained a Bachelor of Science in Business Administration in three years, graduating in 2000. While pursuing her degree, she was enrolled full-time in school to be a barber/stylist. She was born and raised in Oklahoma City, Oklahoma and in 2002, Dallas, Texas became her new home; as of 2016 she moved to Atlanta, GA where she resides with her two daughters who are also authors. TheLynnses.com

Tori Lynn speaks on how her Faith in God caused her to become successful such as enabling her to buy two homes, drive nice cars and travel while only working three days a week. Tori loved the confidence in being able to buy whatever she desired because of an A+ credit rating. She also loved the feeling of being the go-to person when her family needed money. Tori was aware of her highly favored and blessed life.

Losing everything and facing hardship, trials, and tribulations caused the birthing of her autobiography "The Divorce" as she began to write about her experiences while empathizing with others' pain. Tori candidly share both the pain and the loss of her faith in family, man, and God. The thought of suicide became an option, but God; who she later realized had never left her. She wants others to know that God has not left them so, **LIVE**!

www.authortorilynn.com   @AuthorToriLynn

www.ingramcontent.com/pod-product-compliance
Lightning Source LLC
LaVergne TN
LVHW051235080426
835513LV00016B/1598